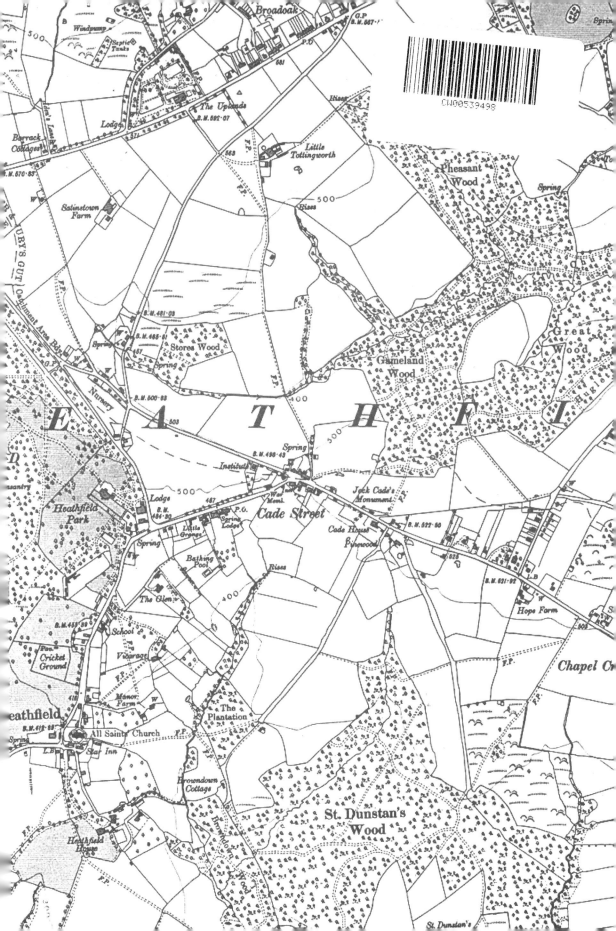

HEATHFIELD
PARK

*A private estate
and a Wealden town*

HEATHFIELD PARK

*A private estate
and a Wealden town*

ROY PRYCE

Published by Roy Pryce, Stone House,
Cade Street, Heathfield TN21 9BS

© Roy Pryce 1996

ISBN 0 9528093 0 3

Design
Melanie Pomfret   Tel 01892 522443

Printing, typesetting and project liaison
Authors' Publishing Guild,
Hadlow Down, East Sussex TN22 4ET
Tel 01825 830319

Cover Photography
Heathfield Park by Leo Kennedy

Inside back cover
Portrait by Jeremy Raj

End papers
Heathfield Park and surrounding area,
Ordnance Survey map, 6 inch, 1932.
(ESRO)

CONTENTS

PREFACE

Those who live in Heathfield sometimes lament the fact that it has no very evident claim to fame. It is almost a hundred years since the first - and up to now the only - substantial history of this corner of the High Weald was published. This began by admitting that Heathfield had not played any great part in the history of the country, and that 'even its few heroes are by adoption'. It did, though, have a unique claim to fame: 'But for Heathfield we should have no official cuckoo'.

This was always a rather fanciful claim, and the Cuckoo Fair which gave rise to the legend has long ceased to be the great local event it once was. But if fame has proved elusive, Heathfield nevertheless has a distinct and interesting past which deserves to be better known and celebrated. Heathfield Park is an important and distinguished part of this, as it is of the local landscape. Its story reaches far back into the history of the area, and provides a continuous link with it over the past seven hundred years.

Early in 1991 developers threatened to build a housing estate on part of the Park. Like many other local residents I was appalled at this prospect, and became an active member of the Friends of Heathfield Park set up at the initiative of Hugh and Sue Wylam to resist it. In between the Public Inquiries which eventually put paid to the developers' plans, I set out to learn more about the history of the Park.

The starting point was *Heathfield Memorials* compiled by Perceval Lucas at the suggestion of his uncle who was then owner of the Park, and published in 1910. This was based in part on the earlier pioneering work of Sylvan Harmer, a member of the distinguished local family. Many of the documents used in that study have been lost, but some - including Humphry Repton's Red Book - are now in the East Sussex Record Office (ESRO) in Lewes. These and the other sources I have used are recorded in the notes at the end of the book.

Many people have helped me with this study. I am particularly grateful to Christopher Whittick, Senior Archivist at ESRO, for his sustained and expert advice, critical encouragement, and detailed comments on an early draft. I have also greatly benefited from the expertise in Sussex history of Colin and Judy Brent, and John Bleach, and about Heathfield itself from Elizabeth Doff, Kay Draycott, Brenda Gardner, Bernard Guile, Joyce Wilkins, and the late Alec Parks.

I have a special debt to the present owners of the Park, Andreas and Inger Ugland for their warm encouragement and generous help. I am grateful too for much useful information to their predecessor, Dr Gerald Moore, and relatives of two earlier owners, Derek Fitzgerald and the late Raymond Clifford-Turner.

Many local residents have also given me invaluable help. I wish to record my warm thanks both to them and others who have helped me with their personal recollections or in other ways, including material for illustrations: Daisy and the late Kenneth Angood, Denise Armstrong, Millie Avard, Ivan Austin, the late Stanley Bayley-Smith, Pamela Bergne-Coupland, Ernest and Catherine Booth, Patrick Burgess, David Calvert, Marjorie Chapman, Audrey Cole, Ruth Cowley, Roland Davis, Jeni Davison, Alan Gillet, Peter Goodwin, Jim Hamper, Stella Hardwick, Graham Harmer, Syd Hopkins, Geoff Hutchinson, Aubrey Knapman, Simon Lamb, Barbara Law, Colin Mackenzie, Norman Marchant, George Mitchell, Raymond Neave, Peter Palmer, Harry Parsons, the late Jack Pennells, Roger Pennington, Ray Pettit, Charles Pledger, Edward Proud, Winifred Read, David Roberts, Charles Robertson, Daphne Robson, Heather Ross, Susan Rowland, Barry Russell, Lucy Skelsey, Geoffrey Smith, Paul Smith, Robin and Joan Thorne, Stella Walker, Robin Wright, and Hugh and Sue Wylam.

I wish also to thank two people in official positions who have been particularly helpful – Ian Kay (Wealden District Council) and Nigel Marshall (East Sussex County Council); Nigel Hamilton and John Scott whose books and expertise I have plundered; Dr Valerie Cromwell, Director of the History of Parliament for permission to use unpublished material on Sir Charles Richard Blunt; Professor Howard A Stutt for (unpaid) research in Ottawa; and the staff of the East Sussex Record Office and the other archives and libraries I have used both in this country and in Canada.

Members of my family have also made important contributions to the book. Susan Pryce and David Griffiths used their librarians' expertise in helping with the research; Charlotte Lipman and Lucy and Jeremy Raj have helped in other ways, and my wife, Sheila, has provided unfailing encouragement and support as well as scrutinising and greatly improving successive drafts.

I am also most grateful to all three members of the local production team – David Brown, Peter Gillies and Melanie Pomfret – for their skills, enthusiasm, and good advice.

I hope the book will contribute to a wider and better appreciation of the history not only of the Park but also of Heathfield itself, and encourage a greater pride in both.

Roy Pryce

Stone House, Cade Street.

Entrance to Heathfield Park

Introduction

1. THE STORY OF THE PARK

For most of its history, Heathfield Park has been a very private place. Tucked away in a quiet corner on the edge of the High Weald in East Sussex, its successive owners have valued it above all for its peace and quiet. In the 1970s part of it became a Wildlife Park for a few years, but otherwise the public has only occasionally been admitted behind the wall which has surrounded it since the early 19th century. The house can be glimpsed through the trees, as can some of the surrounding parkland and the Gibraltar Tower, but the rest is hidden from view.

In recent times, however, the importance of the Park and its house as part of the national heritage have been recognised, and both central and local authorities have garlanded them with honours and taken steps to protect them.

All of the Park has been included within the High Weald Area of Outstanding Natural Beauty, and on English Nature's register of Historic Parks. Part of its ancient woodland, where rare lichens and unusual flora are to be found, has become a Site of Special Scientific Interest. The architectural and historical importance of the house itself, which dates from the late 17th century, has been recognised by its Grade II★ Listed Building status, and the Gibraltar Tower, built in the late 18th century, has not only been listed as a Grade II★ building but also as a scheduled Ancient Monument.

Behind these accolades lies a story which is fascinating from many different points of view. As far as Heathfield is concerned, it is one of the few continuous strands in the history of the area. The owners of the Park and its estate, and the land on which it was created, can now be traced back to the end of the 13th century: they provide a link between the original scattered settlement around the Park and the new town which grew up after the arrival of the railway in 1880. The story of the Park also adds distinction to this quiet corner of the Weald.

At the same time, the successive owners of the estate, and it has had many, provide a remarkable array of personalities and individual histories from a rich variety of backgrounds. Although some of those from more distant times – and, regrettably, almost all their wives – remain rather shadowy figures, several of them have been men of distinction and renown. These include its early noble

The Gibraltar Tower

owners, the Monceux, Fiennes, Dacres and Lennards; General George Eliott, the 'Cock of the Rock' who became a national hero (and the first Lord Heathfield) for his successful defence of Gibraltar during a four-year siege at the end of the 18th century; and his successor, Francis Newbery, a friend of Dr Johnson and his circle, who employed Humphry Repton, the distinguished landscape artist, to advise on the design of the park. It was also during his period as owner that William Turner painted the park, its mansion and the 'Vale of Heathfield' beyond.

For most of the remainder of the 19th century the estate was owned by members of a branch of the Blunt family, which made its initial money out of the South Sea Bubble in the early 18th century. In the present century its owners have included a successful City businessman who was also an early patron of the painter Whistler, two shipowners, a member of the Sassoon family, and a dental surgeon who started out as a child film actor.

But the story of Heathfield Park is more than the sum of its individual owners: it is also part of the economic, social and cultural history of Sussex,

2

and indeed the country at large. Throughout its long history, it has been in a quite remarkable way a faithful mirror of its times. Successive owners have reflected changing patterns of society not only in their own social origins and status and in the various sources of their wealth (and in some cases their ways of losing it) but also their use of the Park and its estate, the changes they have made to the house, and their style of life. It is this which gives the story of the Park more than purely local significance.

NOBLE ORIGINS

The area of land which now forms the Park was originally known as Bayley. For almost four hundred years, from the late 13th century until 1675, it was an outlying part of the Manor of Herstmonceux and was owned by a succession of noble families. Several of these were at the time among the most powerful people in the land: royal courtiers and warriors and holders of high office of state.

For most of this period Bayley was an unenclosed area of forest and heathland, used for hunting and pasture and as a source of timber and wood. But towards the end of the 15th century this part of the Herstmonceux estate became of greater importance as the Wealden iron industry expanded and demand grew for supplies of wood and water. The task of looking after this valuable part of the estate was entrusted to junior members of the family, and a house – it may initially have been a hunting lodge – was built there. Later, as the Heathfield area became the centre for the manufacture of cannon, water from the park helped to drive the machinery which made them.

Early in the 17th century Bayley Park came into existence, surrounded by a ditch and substantial holly hedge (part of which still survives) to keep the deer and other animals in and others out. The Dacre family, for its part, successfully survived the perils of the Civil War - but then succumbed to the pleasures of the Restoration. In 1675 the 24th Lord Dacre, a favourite of Charles II, was forced to sell Bayley to meet his gambling and other debts.

COUNTRY HOUSE AND ESTATE

The Park then ceased to be part of an aristocratic domain. Instead it became the object of desire on the part of a succession of successful self-made men and would-be country gentlemen. Towards the end of the 17th century a splendid mansion was built in the Park. The cost of it ruined its first owner before it was completed, but it greatly added to the allure of the Park. Set in a tranquil spot surrounded by magnificent countryside it commands wonderful views across the valley to the South Downs and the English Channel. The estate is also quite close to the seat of power in London. So there has never been any lack of those wishing to enjoy its pleasures.

The wealth its successive owners needed to buy and maintain it was acquired in many different ways. Some did it through war - either waging it, like General George Eliott - or providing the guns needed for it, like the Fullers. Others made money in more pacific ways through a variety of activities, usually based in London, ranging from business (including publishing and patent medicines), commerce, shipping, and the law. Later on, in the 19th century, the spoils of Empire provided another source of riches, which helped to sustain the Blunt family in ownership for most of that century. Judicious marriages also provided another, and less strenuous, way for some to maintain and increase their resources.

While some of the owners crumpled under the cost of maintaining the house, others - and notably Eliott, Newbery and the Blunts - had sufficient resources to extend the estate. When it was sold off by the Dacres it was under 250 acres: by 1890 it had grown to close to three thousand. But the death that year of Sir Charles William Blunt, the 6th baronet, coincided with a period of agricultural depression and falling land prices. Much of the estate was divided up and sold off.

Although then less than a thousand acres, it continued to attract men of substance from the City. Some of its late Victorian and Edwardian owners, like their predecessors, played a part in local affairs as Justices of the Peace but essentially they were content to live private and domestic lives. They did, however, open the part of the Park around the Gibraltar Tower to the public each August Monday Bank Holiday for the annual show of the Heathfield Amateur and Cottage Gardens Mutual Improvement Society (later the Horticultural Society).

The railway, which arrived in 1880, had a profound effect on the area. A new urban centre - the present Heathfield - grew up at the foot of the hill leading to the Park, much of it on land which had previously belonged to the Heathfield Park estate. The period between the two world wars saw more changes in Heathfield itself than in the Park, with the new settlement as it grew in size and importance taking over the historic name, to distinguish it from what now became known as 'Old' Heathfield. .

During the second world war Sussex again found itself - as during the Napoleonic wars - thrust into the front line. Like many other parks and houses in the region, Heathfield Park was taken over by the War Office and became

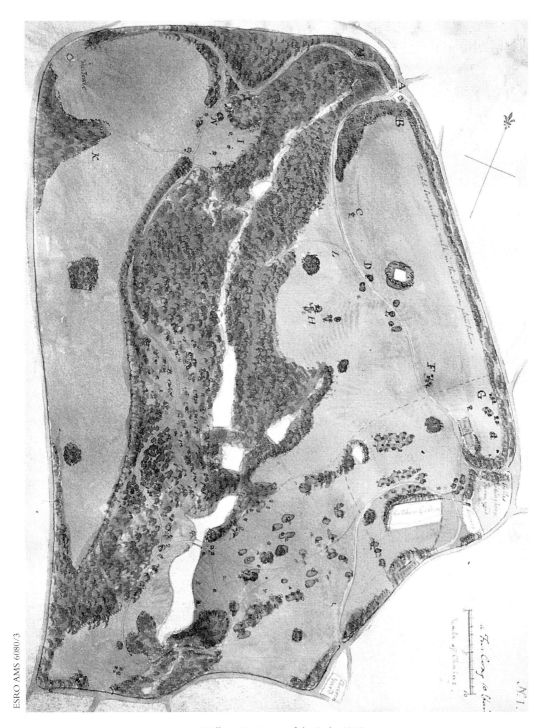

William Figg's map of the Park, 1819

a military encampment. Both Canadian and British troops were stationed there, as well as a communications unit engaged on secret work. It is now known that Lieutenant-General Bernard Montgomery, then Commander of the South-Eastern Army, spent some time there before he was summoned to the Middle East and fame as the victor of El Alamein. Canadian troops stationed in the Park took part in the ill-fated raid on Dieppe, and later it became crammed with troops and equipment in preparation for the liberation of the continent.

RECENT TIMES

Although the house itself suffered considerable damage during its wartime occupation, it was the changes wrought in the aftermath of the war that proved the more lasting and profound.

One of the most important of these was the escalating costs and scarcity of domestic labour. Everywhere these placed great strains on owners of country houses. Heathfield Park, though quite modest in size, was no exception. As elsewhere, its owners sought to meet the increased costs of upkeep by developing new sources of income. A change of ownership in the early sixties brought with it the conversion of part of the park into a Wildlife Park, open to the public. For a while this enjoyed considerable success, though local residents became alarmed when a variety of wild animals escaped and wandered around the district. Conflict with the local authorities also followed as the owner had failed to obtain the necessary planning approval for his initiative.

Subsequently, attempts were made to develop the same area in the western part of the Park, then under corporate rather than private ownership, as a Leisure Park equipped with a 9-hole golf course, holiday chalets and a caravan park, and when this project was temporarily abandoned, as a housing estate. This led to a further series of disputes with the planning authorities and a succession of public enquiries. Local concern about the proposed developments was fuelled both by the new general awareness of environmental issues as well as by worries about the growth of Heathfield itself, and the importance of the Park as a green shield against further urban sprawl. A local amenity society, the Friends of Heathfield Park, came into being to give voice to these concerns.

It is this conflict between private and public interests which provides a major theme of the history of the Park over the last thirty years. But the developers were repulsed, and in 1993 Inger and Andreas Ugland bought the eastern part of the Park with its mansion as a family residence, and acquired the rest

View along the veranda

early in 1996, thus reuniting and restoring to private ownership the whole of the Park within its 19th century walls. For the first time in its history the Park has Norwegian owners: another significant reflection of changing times, and of our closer ties with the rest of Europe.

Looking back over the past seven hundred years, it is remarkable how faithfully the history of the Park has reflected the many changes in both local and national circumstances. It is also remarkable that the Park and its house have survived both these, and many changes in ownership, relatively unscathed. When it last changed hands in 1993 Heathfield Park was described as 'the epitome of an impressive small estate'. Now that it is protected by the vigilance of public authorities, both national and local, there is good hope that it will long continue to grace the Wealden countryside.

ROGER PENNINGTON

Lakeside in the Park

A Manorial Outpost (c. 1300-1675)

2. THE SETTING: HEATHFIELD

It is difficult today to imagine what Heathfield was like before the arrival of the railway and the motor car. But it is not impossible. The best place at which to try is Cade Street, the hamlet on the ridge at the eastern end of the town on the road to Battle. Looking south across what Turner called - inaccurately - the 'Vale of Heathfield' to the South Downs the scene is still recognisably the same as when he painted it. On a good day, the sun glints in the distance on the waters of the Channel towards Pevensey Bay, where William the Conqueror landed in 1066. The land between is a patchwork of small fields, still quite heavily wooded, with a scattering of farms and houses. In the foreground the spire of the parish church at Old Heathfield rises above the denser woodland in and around Heathfield Park. The land then continues its climb up to the ridge where Cade Street stands, almost 500 feet above sea level, marking the southern boundary of the High Weald.

It is here that the original settlement was located. But, like others in the Weald, it was a straggle of a place, not a neat village. Travellers came along this way long before any settlers arrived. They used the ridgeway to skirt around the dark recesses of the great inland forest of the Andredsweald. It ran in an almost straight east-west line for twenty-eight miles between what are now Rye and Uckfield. Clinging to a succession of ridges it provided a relatively hard and dry surface amid the surrounding sticky clay, and had the additional advantage of crossing only two insignificant runnels of water along the way.[1]

Three other routeways converged in the area, one running north-east towards Hawkhurst, one going north in the direction of Tunbridge Wells, and another to the south towards Pevensey. These were used from the earliest times by hunters, and from around the sixth century BC by those who began to exploit the iron ore which was discovered in the Weald. They were joined about the middle of the first century BC by the Belgae from the lower Rhineland. These new arrivals developed a substantial production of iron in the Battle-Sedlescombe area: early bloomeries probably dating from this period have also been found at Dallington and at Turners Green near Warbleton. This activity was continued and further developed by the Romans

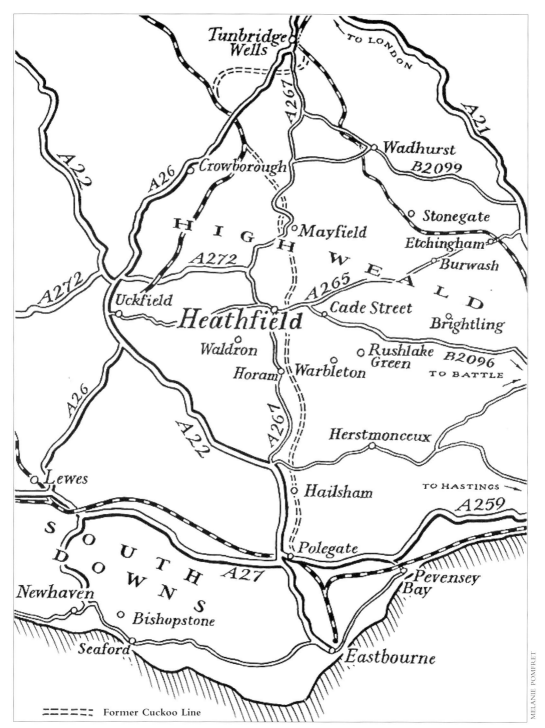

Map of Heathfield district

who arrived in the middle of the first century AD and who used the resultant slag to provide better surfaces for the transport of the finished products.[2]

We know that Romans used the ridgeways in the Heathfield area from some fragments of pottery and glass which have been found there. But neither then nor later did these become major routes. As today, people preferred whenever possible to go along by the coast: it was faster and safer. Even after the arrival of the turnpike roads in the middle of the 18th century the wild, windswept heathland along the ridges remained dangerous country for travellers, the haunt of robbers, highwaymen and smugglers. For many centuries the Weald was regarded as lying beyond the bounds of the civilised world.

EARLY SETTLERS

The Saxons, however, who arrived in Sussex towards the middle of the 5th century began to push inland, probably under pressure from an increasing population.

Much of the story of what has been called a 'major act of colonisation' remains shrouded in mystery, but by the eighth and ninth centuries large tracts of the Weald belonged either to royal or church estates based on the Downs. The first stage of development probably consisted of the seasonal movement of swine up into the beech forests on the southern slopes of the Weald – many of these droveways can still be traced in today's lanes. The erection of temporary shelters followed, leading to more permanent clearing and occupation.[3]

From an early stage, land at Heathfield was owned by the Manor of Bishopstone which at the time of Edward the Confessor (1042-66) belonged to the Bishop of Selsey: it remained in the possession of his successors when the bishopric was transferred to Chichester sometime before 1086.

A document dating from the middle of the 13th century records that the Manor of Bishopstone had woodlands at Heathfield. This land could well have formed the nucleus of what later became the Manor of Heathfield, which remained attached to Bishopstone until the middle of the 14th century, and part of the possessions of the Bishop of Chichester until the mid 16th century. We do not know how extensive an area this covered but there are records also from the mid 13th century of those holding land at Heathfield from this Manor. From these it is clear that it had been parcelled out in small holdings among many different individuals. Other manors also held land in the area, so from a very early stage ownership of land in the Heathfield area was very fragmented. This was a characteristic which was to persist through and beyond the medieval period. There was no single Lord of the Manor to subject the inhabitants of the

area to his will. Nor did any single landowner subsequently emerge as a dominant figure in the Heathfield area, though successive owners of Heathfield Park,
as well as others, certainly nourished the ambition to become so.[4]

The clearing and settlement of the High Weald was a lengthy process
which continued after the Norman conquest. The areas which were habit-
ually used for pasturing acquired names long before they became permanent
settlements: examples of this include Mayfield, Cuckfield and Ninfield.
Heathfield is another case in point. The name is of Saxon origin, a compound
of 'haep' and 'feld' meaning a stretch of uncultivated open land in the Weald.
This suggests that it was during the Saxon period that regular pasturing developed in the area: it does not by itself however provide a secure basis for dating
the development of permanent settlement. In any case this was a gradual and
very scattered process. The area did not provide any obvious site with over-
whelmingly good defensive characteristics: nor was its location of any
significant strategic importance. So there were no compelling reasons for
habitations to cluster together. The major routes, both east-west and north-
south, lay elsewhere. It was along them that armies marched and battles were
fought. There may once have been a bloody encounter at a site long known
as 'Slaughter Common' (later part of the Heathfield Park estate) but otherwise the Heathfield area was a quiet and rather remote spot on the edge of
the High Weald.[5]

ON THE EDGE OF THINGS

From the beginning the area was on the edge of things in other ways, too.
Geographically it straddled the watershed between the land draining
south into the Cuckmere valley and the northern-facing slopes draining into
the valley of the Rother. It was in Sussex - but the border with Kent was
only a few miles away, while the centres of both secular and ecclesiastical
power in Sussex were far away.

When the Anglo-Saxons first created a framework of royal administration and justice, the area was divided between different jurisdictions. The
boundary between them ran through the middle of the land which was later
to become Heathfield Park: curiously, but significantly, the same line corre-
sponds quite closely to the way the ownership of the Park was split in the
1980s. The eastern part was allocated to the township of Tottingworth in
the Hundred of Hawkesborough, while the western part was assigned to the
township of Isenhurst in the Hundred of Dill. Later on, under the Normans,
that same line also became the frontier between two of the larger and more

important administrative units into which Sussex was divided – the Rape of Hastings and the Rape of Pevensey.[6]

From the point of view of the church authorities also the Heathfield area was – and was to remain – very much an outpost. It was quite distant from what were to become the great monastic centres of Battle and Lewes, and well to the north of the route which connected them. And it did not itself attract a religious community, unlike Michelham or Warbleton, for instance, each of which became the site of an Augustinian priory.

PETER PALMER

View from Cade Street today

The peripheral nature of the location set a pattern which has persisted to the present day. The railway, for instance, arrived at Heathfield only very late in the 19th century and long after most other places in the south-east had been connected with it, in part because Heathfield lay on the edge of areas controlled by two rival railway companies. (Later on, it was also one of the first places to lose its railway line). The new town created by the railway then found itself, as it developed, stretching across the boundary dividing the two parishes of Heathfield and Waldron, with its affairs split between different local authorities. This was a problem it took almost eighty years to resolve.

Today Heathfield is still on the edge of things in almost every way. The most graphic illustration of this is to be found in the Ordnance Survey maps: the national grid splits the area into no less than four fragments each on the corner of a separate section. Even in other contexts, where Heathfield is at least treated as a unit, it is usually consigned to the outer limits of an organisational area - this is true, for instance, for parliamentary elections, local government, and the provision of public utilities - such as water, gas, electricity and telecommunications (each of which assigns the town to a different area). Rather typically, Heathfield was also one of the few places in the kingdom the National Lottery failed to reach when it was launched late in 1994.

But although there clearly are disadvantages attached to being on the periphery of things, there have always been considerable advantages too.

Distance from centres of power has always meant greater freedom to get on with your own affairs. In the case of Heathfield, which had no dominant local lord either, this bred a sturdy independence of mind and action among the local population. For many centuries this meant a good deal of lawlessness, but it was also the ground which nurtured the local Protestant martyrs - two of whom came from Cade Street - and the later religious Nonconformity which has remained strong in the area. Today, distance has other advantages, not least the relative tranquillity which Heathfield enjoys away from motorways and the urban sprawl that blights so much of the Sussex coast, as well as swift access to the surrounding countryside.

THE PATTERN OF SETTLEMENT

Just as the original siting of the settlement had important long-term consequences for Heathfield, so too did its early configuration. In this the choice of location for the church played a significant part. It was certainly not the most obvious site, being neither on nor close to the junction of the ancient routeways, nor was it at the highest point in the locality. The chosen place may have been an ancient pagan place of worship, hidden away in the woods. But the spot does command good views to the south, and this may have been the decisive factor as those who made it a Christian place of worship certainly came from that direction. At all events, the fact that it was some distance from

ROGER PENNINGTON

All Saints Church and the Star Inn

the main routes of the area meant that it did not become the focus of a village - unlike the churches at Burwash, Etchingham and Mayfield, for instance. A few dwellings and eventually an inn clustered around it, but these remained distinct and apart from the scatter of houses along the ridgeways.

We cannot be certain when a church was first built at Heathfield: it is possible that like Mayfield it was during the Saxon period, but there is no surviving evidence of this. The first written record dates from 1148, so it may be that it was built as part of the new wave of of church buildings following the Norman Conquest which included others in more remote places in the Weald such as Ardingly, Balcombe, Cuckfield, West Hoathly and Wivelsfield. What is known is that the church at Heathfield was linked with that of Bishopstone, which accords with the other links known to have existed with the manor there.[7]

Active clearance was still going on in the area in the first half of the 13th century. It was then that the parish church may have been rebuilt and enlarged. Then, as now, it consisted of a nave and aisles (in addition to a south chancel and crypt) which provided space for 2-300 worshippers. It was clearly designed to serve a substantial, if scattered, community.

15

The Cuckoo Fair at Cade Street, early 20th century

THE MID 13TH CENTURY

Records of the Manor of Bishopstone provide some idea of the size of the settlement in the Heathfield area by the middle of the 13th century. In addition to the church and its vicar there was a watermill, three houses, and three workshops (for craftsmen such as blacksmiths and carpenters), one of them next to the churchyard. We also have details of 43 people living in the area, the land they held, and their manorial obligations. If we include those attached to other manors in the district – such as Runtington, Sapperton and Tottingworth – and add in their dependents and others, the total population of the parish may have amounted to a couple of hundred or more.[8]

This was very small in comparison with some neighbouring settlements. Wadhurst, for instance, probably had a population in the region of a thousand by the end of the century. But the growing importance of the settlement and activity in the area was both recognised and given an important boost early in the 14th century. In 1315 the Bishop of Chichester succeeded in obtaining from Edward II the grant of a weekly market and an annual fair at Heathfield. The market was to be held each Thursday; the three-day fair on the feast of St Richard to commemorate Richard de Wych, bishop of Chichester from 1244 to 1253 who was canonised in 1262.

It is this fair which became an important local event and with which the Cuckoo Fair legend is associated. But the story of both fair and legend is far from simple.

It is not certain, for instance, when the fair was originally held. By the end of the 13th century there were two days in the liturgical year associated with St Richard – 3 April (feast of the Deposition, recalling his death) and 14 June (feast of the Translation of his relics). One source claims that there were two annual fairs from the beginning: another that there was only one, and in June rather than April. By the end of the 17th century there were certainly two annual fairs, in April and June. After 1752, when a new calendar was introduced, the original dates were changed to 14 April and 27 June, and in the early 19th century the June fair was moved to 16 October.

Both became known as 'Cuckoo' fairs though this name was associated more particularly with that held in April, a local legend claiming that it was here that an old woman released a cuckoo from her basket to herald the arrival of Spring. It is impossible to know when or how this legend originated – it is one of a number related to the appearance of the cuckoo, some of which are deeply embedded in mythology – though the earliest reference to the Heathfield version dates only from the early 19th century. It was later celebrated and made more widely known in a poem by Rudyard Kipling, and further elaborated by the claim made in the introduction to *Heathfield*

Among the Pines: near Heathfield High Street in the 1930s

Memorials that it was Heathfield's privilege 'every year to announce that Spring is here'.[9]

This was pure romantic invention: but at least the fairs were real and a major local event. Eighteenth century maps show 'Heathfield Fair Place' close by what is now the site of Heathfield Community College at Cade Street. It was there and along the road itself that the Cuckoo Fair was still being held this century up until the second world war, and where most of the shops, inns and traders were to be found before the railway arrived. Some additional buildings were erected close to the church - including the one which is now the Star public house. It is claimed, though on uncertain evidence, that this dates from 1348 when the church was rebuilt after a fire: it may originally have been put up to house visiting clergy from Bishopstone. But there is no doubt that the main settlement remained along and around the ridgeway. Until the late 18th century this was known as 'Catte Street' and in late 16th century maps was shown as being as, or more prominent than 'Heathfield', the settlement around the church. One of its functions was to provide places for alcoholic refreshment: over the years these have included the Cat and Shoulder of Mutton, the Blacksmiths Arms, the Crown, the Half Moon, and (today) the Jack Cade.[10]

The first documents relating to 'Bayley' - the tract of land at Heathfield which was later to become the site of Heathfield Park and which may have been named after an early owner - date from just before the grant of the market and fair. It is clear that there was by then a flourishing little community in the area. But the early 14th century marked the high point of its development for some time, for in 1348/9 the Black Death arrived in Sussex and up to half of the county's population died within a few months. The area under cultivation was reduced, and woodland encroached upon medieval fields. A long period of economic depression set in which lasted until the end of the 15th century when new technology led to a major expansion of the iron industry in the Weald, and not least in the Heathfield area itself.[11]

3. THE HERSTMONCEUX CONNECTION: THE MONCEUX, FIENNES AND DACRES

Alleged misconduct by a cleric in the early 14th century provides the first documentary evidence about Bayley, the area of land at Heathfield which was later to become the site of Heathfield Park.

On 17 April 1327 the Court of the Manor of Herstmonceux was told that Geoffrey de Eton, prebendary of Heathfield at Chichester cathedral, had illegally occupied the tenement which belonged to Richard le Hostiler 'at Baille'. The court ordered that he should be arrested and brought before it to justify his action and do fealty to the Lord of the Manor.[1]

At its next meeting on 25 September, the rector did not appear in person but sent his servant. He brought with him a legal document showing that the rector had every right to occupy the building because he had acquired it from Custance, the widow of Richard le Hostiler. The deed also showed that the 6½ acres of land in Heathfield, together with the buildings and trees standing on it, had been jointly acquired by Custance and her late husband from John de Monceux, Lord of the Manor of Herstmonceux. On behalf of the rector it was acknowledged that he owed the Manor 2/2d a year for this land: he was ordered to appear to do fealty at the next session of the court 'and save his default'.

This was not, however, the end of the affair. Geoffrey de Eton failed to appear at the December meeting of the court: it ordered that he should be arrested for non-payment of dues and 'many defaults'. It may be that he was by now a sick man: at all events the court was told at its sitting on 30 May the following year that he had died and that his brother and heir, Thomas de Eton, had sold the house and land at Bayley to the new vicar of Heathfield, John de Assbourne. He duly appeared to do fealty and was assessed for his manorial rent - though like his predecessor he was soon to get into trouble with the court on other matters.[2]

These early documents about Bayley now allow us to trace its history much further back than in the account given by Perceval Lucas in his *Heathfield Memorials*, which says that 'Bayley was commonly reputed parcel of the Manor of Hurstmonceux' but dates the beginning of the connection only from the middle of the 15th century. This was based on speculation that Sir Thomas Dacre then acquired Bayley through marriage to a descendent of the Pierpoint family of Hurstpierpoint. We now know that this account was in part based on a false trail: Bayley had been held by successive owners of the

Manor of Herstmonceux at least since the end of the 13th century, and the Dacre connection began only through the marriage of one of Sir Thomas's daughters.[3]

We cannot be certain when land at Heathfield was first acquired by the family which owned the Manor of Herstmonceux. It may have been at an early stage in the process of the opening up of the Weald when, as we have seen, other manors on its southern fringes acquired a stake in the area for seasonal pasturing of pigs and other animals. We do know that in 1292 John de Monceux, Lord of the Manor of Herstmonceux held 200 acres of land from the Manor of Laughton as a free tenant. A survey of the manor dated 13 November of that year shows that in addition to its demesne at Laughton itself – later to become the seat of the Pelham family – the manorial lands, some of which may have been held of the Manor of Bishopstone, stretched in a north-north-easterly direction as far as Possingworth with a detached area in Waldron and the western part of Heathfield. It is a reasonable assumption from the evidence of the Court Rolls of the Manor of Herstmonceux thirty-five years later that part, if not all, of the 200 acres held by John de Monceux were at Heathfield, and included the land and buildings at Bayley.[4]

The Manor of Herstmonceux itself had been given after the Norman Conquest to William, the son of Robert, Earl of Eu. But soon afterwards another noble family called de Herst had taken over, and adopted the surname of Monceux. Early in the thirteenth century one of the members of the family had become constable of Pevensey Castle, and his son took a prominent part on the side of Simon de Montfort in his struggle with Henry III which included the battle of Lewes in 1264, when the king was heavily defeated.[5]

THE FIENNES

In the early years of the 14th century the last of the male Monceux died without children, and the family lands passed to his sister, Maud de Monceux. She married Sir John de Fiennes, the son of another distinguished noble family of Anglo-Norman origins which then began a long association of more than three hundred and fifty years with the Manor of Herstmonceux.

The Fiennes family was to become for several centuries one of the most notable in the south of England. Its rise to wealth, influence and political power gathered momentum as the 14th century progressed. William Fiennes, who succeeded when he was 21, played his part by marrying the daughter and heiress of Geoffrey, Lord Say. Although his eldest son died when only seventeen, his brother William continued the family's ascent by marrying another heiress, Elizabeth Batsford, through whom he acquired large estates in Dallington, Wartling and adjoining parishes in Sussex. He was knighted and also served for two years as Sheriff, dying in 1405.[6]

During the lifetimes of these Fiennes we have only sparse information about what was going on at Bayley, though it is clear that its woodland and heath were being used by those living locally. From the point of view of the owners of the Manor of Herstmonceux, however, it was very much an outlying possession and not, it would seem, greatly prized at the time.

A list of the rents being paid to the manor dating from around 1340 shows that 'a barbed arrow' – the equivalent today of a peppercorn rent – was all that was due from those using wood at Bayley and on the surrounding heathland for fuel and hedging. The rent for land there was similarly modest. 'Philipus atte Esthouse' was liable for a rent for the house which had been the inn, and others for the use of heathland or commons at 'Baile'. A list of customary duties from the same period also made mention of fetching two cartloads of wood from 'as far afield as Bayley' – a service which was worth 3d and a meal.[7]

In 1379 an argument erupted over some land at Bayley and was brought before the manorial court. The trouble arose on the death of John Notebroun of Bayley when his land was claimed both

Brass memorial to Sir William Fiennes in All Saints, Herstmonceux

by William Mirefield – who said he had a charter from the lord of the manor – and Notebroun's relative and heir Agnes Hereward. The Fiennes seemed to have resolved the matter by taking the land back into their own hands, and then letting it out to a farmer.[8]

By then Sussex, like much of the rest of the country, was suffering severely from the effects of the Black Death. There was widespread poverty and discontent and a refusal to provide feudal services, which were now increasingly commuted into money payments. At Heathfield itself there is evidence that not only had clearance of new land come to a halt, but also that woodland was again encroaching on land which had previously been cultivated. The Weald as a whole was noted for its lawlessness, its remoter parts being out of reach of any authority. And at the same time there was a constant threat of raids from the French, and in 1380 a fear of invasion from across the Channel.[9]

In 1399 Henry of Lancaster seized power from Richard II, the last of the Plantagenets, whom he speedily put to death. His family owned extensive lands in Sussex, including a huge area of Ashdown Forest, and the Fiennes became prominent supporters and officials of the dynasty he founded. Both of the sons of Sir Roger Fiennes fought in the French wars with Henry V, and held high positions in the court of his successor, Henry VI. The younger of the two, James, served as Sheriff of Kent in 1437 and of Surrey and Sussex in 1439, was summoned to Parliament in 1446/7, and was made a Baron, adopting the title of Lord Saye and Sele. He subsequently became Lord Chamberlain, a member of the King's Council, and for the last year of his life, Lord Treasurer. He was one of the most powerful men in the land.

Herstmonceux Castle

His elder brother Roger inherited the family estates in 1405 when he was 16. He fought in several campaigns in France, including the battle of Agincourt. Like his brother he served Henry VI under whom he became Treasurer of the Household, and in 1440 obtained the King's permission to fortify the manor house at Herstmonceux, converting it into the imposing brick-built castle which we know today.[10]

ENTER THE DACRES

A few years later, in 1446, Sir Roger Fiennes negotiated a rather unusual marriage agreement for his two sons, Richard and Robert. It was with Sir Thomas Dacre of Hurstpierpoint, a member of a distinguished family originating in Cumberland which had been enobled by Edward III in 1321. Sir Thomas had two daughters. Richard was contracted to marry Joan Dacre(then about 13 years old) and Robert to marry her sister Philippa. A curious feature of the agreement was that rather than requiring dowries to accompany the brides, Sir Roger agreed to pay Thomas Dacre for his daughters: 200 marks for Joan and 250 for Philippa. He also undertook 'to fetche the syde dowghters to London atte his own costes'. The agreement required that a rival suitor for Joan, John Fyloll – with whom a marriage contract had been signed in November the previous year – 'be not lett to see the seide Johane and there with her to speke'.[11]

The explanation for this apparently one-sided arrangement probably lay in the expectation that in the course of time Joan Dacre would inherit the land and possessions of both branches of the Dacre family: not only those of 'the Dacres of the South' through her father but also, through her grandfather, those of the northern branch of the family which had remained in Cumberland. This in fact came about in 1457, eleven years after her marriage to Richard Fiennes, and greatly increased – yet again – the Herstmonceux family's fortunes. Nor was that all, for the following year, in November 1458, Richard obtained permission from Henry VI to assume the Dacre title. It was a name that was to be associated with Bayley for the next two hundred years.[12]

THE JACK CADE STORY

In the meantime, however, tragedy had overtaken Richard's brother, Lord Saye and Sele, as a result of his growing unpopularity. The agent of his undoing was Jack Cade who raised a rebellion against Henry VI and his circle in 1450. As Cade is associated in a number of ways both with Heathfield and the Dacres this is a convenient point at which to examine both the claims and the continuing controversy surrounding them.

Cade's rebellion originated in Kent and took place against a background of economic and social discontent which generated widespread support also in Sussex and Essex. In July 1450 the rebels, who had marched on the capital and set up camp at Blackheath, sent the King a letter in which they demanded that he should remove his ministers and reform the government, repeal the Statute of Labourers, and control the taxing power of the sheriffs. The King responded

NEAR THIS SPOT
WAS SLAIN THE NOTORIOUS REBEL
JACK CADE
BY ALEXANDER IDEN ESQ.
SHERIFF OF KENT A D 1450

HIS BODY WAS CARRIED TO LONDON
AND HIS HEAD FIXED UPON LONDON BRIDGE

Monument to Jack Cade

by sending an armed force against them, but this was defeated at Sevenoaks. The rebels occupied the City of London, forced the king and his courtiers to flee, and began proceedings against a number of those they denounced as traitors and extortioners, most notably Lord Saye and Sele. He was taken to the Guildhall, condemned, and summarily beheaded. Later that day his naked corpse was dragged behind a horse through the streets of the City. A number of others met a similar fate. Widespread looting of the City followed during the next two days.

A bloody battle for control of Southwark bridge followed on the evening of Sunday 5 July between Cade's followers and royal troops from the Tower assisted by loyal Londoners. By morning the charred and smoking bridge was littered with dead bodies: several hundred had perished in the battle. A truce was called and negotiations began to persuade the rebels to withdraw. A general pardon was offered in the name of the Queen, and accepted. But as far as Cade was concerned this was speedily withdrawn on the grounds that he had given a false name: as on other occasions he called himself John Mortimer, which firmly identified him with the King's great rival, Richard Duke of York.

With a small band of followers Cade made off for northern Kent, passing through Dartford, where he made an abortive attempt to take Queenborough castle. On 10 July a writ for his arrest as a traitor was issued, with a reward of 1000 marks for his head. He was pursued by a posse of men led by Alexander Iden, Sheriff of Kent, who according to some reports followed him into Sussex and finally caught up with him on 12 July at Heathfield. Cade is supposed to have taken refuge in Newick House, a moated farm house later known as 'Cade's Castle' – part of the moat can still be seen. He was shot and captured when he emerged for a game of bowls in the garden of a tavern on the south side of the road at the top of Catte Street. Cade was badly injured: he died as he was taken back to London, where his head was displayed on London Bridge.

This account of his capture has, however, always been contested. A number of contemporary sources assert that it occurred not at Heathfield but at Hothfield in Kent, a few miles north-west of Ashford. It is this version which Shakespeare used in Henry VI, Part II. A substantial literature has grown up on the issue and historians remain divided about it.

Part of the argument concerns Cade's earlier connections with the area and with Sir Thomas Dacre. Whether or not Cade was a Sussex man is in dispute: the name was a common one in the neighbourhood but there is continuing uncertainty about Cade's origins. It is generally accepted, however, that Cade spent some time in the service of Sir Thomas Dacre at Hurstpierpoint where Sir Thomas was Lord of the Manor and that during this period he murdered a pregnant woman and was forced to flee the country between December 1448 and December 1449. The claim that Sir Thomas subsequently became one of his supporters is however hard to believe, not only because of Cade's criminal record, but also – and above all – because of his leading part in the execution of Lord Saye and Sele, the most prominent member of the Fiennes family into which Sir Thomas had married his daughter. Nor would his son-in-law have sought permission from Henry VI to assume the Dacre title had the family name become associated with the failed rebel.

The rival claims to the place where Cade was captured are more problematic. The chroniclers are divided on the subject, and there is no decisive evidence in favour of either of the two claimants. The proximity of Hothfield to Ashford, which was at the heart of the rising, lends some credence to its claim if it is assumed either that Cade was seeking to rally his supporters or was fleeing to the continent. As far as Heathfield is concerned, it was certainly not on a direct route had escape to the continent been his intention – but it too was in an area where he had supporters: two of them at Brightling are quoted as having said openly that 'the Kynge was a naterell foole'. In Heathfield's favour are also the strength and persistence of the local associations, including 'Cade's Castle' and 'Iden's Lane' which connects it with the spot in Cade Street where he is supposed to have been captured. But local legend also owes a great deal to a later owner of Heathfield Park, Francis Newbery, who deliberately chose to celebrate and perpetuate the Cade connection for his own purposes as a way of proving his devotion to law and order at a time of revolution, and of adding historical lustre to Heathfield, its Park and – by extension – to himself. However, that and the change of name from Catte to Cade Street only came almost three hundred and fifty years after the event. On the truth of the Cade story, the jury is still out.[13]

PETER PALMER

Pub sign at Cade Street

4. BAYLEY WOOD AND BAYLEY PARK:
THE LENNARDS

A new phase in the history of Bayley began around the end of the 15th century. This was closely related to the changes taking place in the locality at that time which witnessed a major development of activity in the Weald, and especially its iron industry. What up to then had been a very peripheral part of the estate now became much more important as a result of the new demand for the wood and water needed for the industry as well as timber for other purposes. As a result, the owners of Bayley now began to take a much closer interest in exploiting its resources.

WEALDEN IRON INDUSTRY

Technological changes coupled with increased demand were the main driving forces behind the resurgence of the local iron industry. The most important technical innovation was the introduction of the blast furnace from France to replace the traditional crude bloomery method of making iron. This meant that production could now be a more continuous process, the quantity produced greater, and the quality higher. A second, but earlier innovation, was the use of the forge hammer, driven by water power. This made the working of the pig iron easier and also widened the range of products. Later on, a third innovation was to prove of particular importance for the Heathfield area. This was the use of moulds for the making of heavy cannon, rather than assembling them from bands of iron. The first successful use of this new method is generally ascribed to Ralph Hogge of Buxted in 1543: it meant a more reliable and safer product, as well as one that could be produced in greater quantities than before.

Heathfield and its surrounding district became a major centre for this reinvigorated industry. Fields were scoured for deposits of iron ore and the production of pig iron from bloomeries was now augmented by the building of blast furnaces. The Pelham family established one at Waldron; there was another near Burwash Common, and the Fullers later built one at Heathfield itself. There were also several forges in the district, including Glaziers at Brightling and Bibleham at Mayfield.

Bayley itself was not a suitable site for either furnace or forge, being too high up on the ridge to generate sufficient head of water to operate them successfully. But it did have at least two of the three raw materials needed for the

Traces of an earlier house in the basement of Heathfield Park
(From a drawing by W C Alexander)

industry. There is no evidence of iron ore itself having been found in any quantity at the site, but it certainly had ample supplies of both wood and water. These now needed careful management, and it was no doubt to provide this that the Dacres took a closer interest in this part of their estate.

According to the *Heathfield Memorials*, the first house on the site 'is supposed to have been built' in the time of Henry VII (1485-1509). It is not known where or what sort of a house it was, although there is some evidence of an earlier building on the site of the present house and part of its basement may date from that period, and could have been its chapel. It is known that members of the Dacre family were living at Bayley from the late 16th century, and they may have been there earlier. One piece of evidence that might have shed light on this – a brass to the memory of a lady of the Fiennes family discovered in Heathfield church at the beginning of the 19th century – has unfortunately long since gone missing.[1]

IMPACT OF THE TUDORS

What is known is that this was a period of fluctuating political fortune for the Dacres. Up to that point they had shown a remarkable capacity for political survival, having successfully switched their allegiance from the Lancastrian Henry VI to his Yorkist successor Edward IV, while retaining royal favour. Dealing with the Tudors, however, proved a much tougher proposition. Although one Dacre held royal appointments under Henry VIII, and also attended him at the Field of the Cloth of Gold in 1520, he later fell out of favour and was thrown into the Fleet prison in 1525 charged with collusion with thieves 'knowinge them to have commytted felonye and dyvers other his misdoings'.[2]

He was soon restored to royal favour but his successor, another Thomas, fared much worse. In 1536 the King brought an important test case against him in his Chancery Court. This concerned the practice of 'uses' – a device to avoid payment of inheritance dues to a feudal superior. The King was greatly concerned about the loss of royal revenue by this means, and was determined to make Dacre an example. He put great pressure on the judges to obtain a favourable outcome of the case – and Dacre duly lost.[3]

Having suffered this blow, Thomas Fiennes then became involved, a few years later, in a fatal misadventure. On the night of 30 April 1541 he set off with a group of friends on a poaching expedition to Laughton Park, owned by Thomas Pelham. Some of them were intercepted, and in the course of an

*Sir Thomas Fynes,
Lord Dacre*

affray one of Pelham's servants was killed. The whole party was indicted on a charge of murder. Although Thomas Fiennes protested his innocence he was brought to trial, and Henry VIII turned aside the judges' pleas for mercy. Lord Dacre was hanged at Tyburn on 30 June 1541.[4]

His son, Gregory Fiennes, worked hard to restore the family fortunes. In about 1543 he contracted a promising marriage with Anne Sackville, a member of one of the most distinguished and powerful families in the region. Her brother Thomas, later Lord Buckhurst, was a man of great ability and ambition who was to become one of the favourites of Queen Elizabeth and her Lord Treasurer. Gregory Fiennes himself succeeded in 1559 in recovering the titles which had been forfeited by his father. But he was forced to sell off parts of the estate, and Herstmonceux itself was badly neglected and fell into disrepair.[5]

Sampson Lennard

EXPLOITING BAYLEY

Having failed to profit from the massive redistribution of land which occurred during the Tudor period, particularly as a result of the dissolution of the monasteries, the Dacres had to husband their resources.

This may well have have been the motive behind their decision to undertake a survey of the Herstmonceux estate in 1569. They needed an accurate analysis of its resources, and their potential, particularly in the light of the very rapid expansion of the Wealden iron industry which was then taking place. Between 1548 and 1574 the number of ironworks of all kinds more than doubled. This meant a greatly increased demand for charcoal to charge the blast furnaces: its price quadrupled between 1540 and 1600. The coppiced wood used in its production was also in great demand. This added to other pressures on the supply of wood, and brought in its train a sharp rise in its price in the last two decades of the century. So owners of woodland had every incentive to establish what they owned, and to take steps to improve the management of their estates, and in particular their woodland.[6]

It is in the context of this survey that we find a specific reference to Bayley Wood:[7]

> 'There is in the parish of Hethfylde a Wood called Bayly Wood contg 107 acres in ye tenure of ye Lord of Buckhurst wch was stored with goodly Timber trees of Oke and Byche whereof the one half is fallen by the Ld of Buckhurst and his father, and the residue is yearly to be felled, without preserving the Copices, by my Lord Dacres Grant and Sale of the same Woods'.

It is clear from this that Bayley Wood was now prized for its 'goodly timber trees'. The Dacres appear to have sold the timber on it, perhaps for a period of years, to Lord Buckhurst, who was now a close relative. Buckhurst clearly had his eyes on the Heathfield area, no doubt in the hope of sharing in the profits from its industrial boom, for some years later, in 1588, he became Lord of the Manor of Heathfield buying it off two middle-men shortly after they had purchased it from Queen Elizabeth. She had acquired it in July 1561 when the See of Chichester became vacant.[8]

The growing importance of the woodland at Bayley in the late 16th century and its owners' concern to establish clearly their rights over it are also reflected in a dispute with Thomas Pelham. This rather typical piece of Tudor litigation followed closely after the survey of the Dacre estate – and may indeed have arisen from it. The Pelhams were a long-established Sussex family who had come to prominence under the Lancastrians. Sir John Pelham had supported their bid for power, and had been knighted by Henry IV shortly after he ascended the throne in 1399. He subsequently served as a royal sword-bearer and Constable of Pevensey Castle. It was he who also much enlarged the family estate, which by the early 15th century included the manors of Burwash and

Margaret Fynes

Laughton. The Dacre's land at Bayley was held from these two manors: a document which probably dates from the middle of the 16th century shows that an annual rent of 2 shillings was then being paid to the manor of Laughton, while a pound of cummin was due to the manor of Burwash.[9]

Although we do not know how the dispute arose, much can be inferred from the terms in which it was resolved in 1575/6. The award which, significantly, more than doubled the money rent payable to the manor of Laughton declared: [10]

> 'that Sampson Lennard esqre and Lady Dacres shall for ever herafter hold all those lands called Baylye lyeing in Heathfield and Burwash of Thomas Pelham esqre and his heirs and assigns by fealty and 5s per annum and one pound of cummin as they are and have been holden'.

It appears from this that although Gregory Fiennes was still alive, control over Bayley had passed to his sister Margaret and her husband, Sampson Lennard of Chevening in Kent, whom she had married in 1564. It is possible that they may also have been living at Bayley, though when Margaret inherited the Herstmonceux estate in 1594 it is there they went to live. They had seven sons and six daughters; maintained a staff of some 25 servants; and were noted for their 'noble housekeeping and hospitality'. After several years' legal battles she was eventually recognised as Baroness Dacre, and her husband served as High Sheriff for Kent in 1590 and also sat in several Parliaments. But there was a price to be paid: they lived beyond their means and began to dissipate their great possessions.[11]

CREATION OF BAYLEY PARK

Only occasional references to Bayley are to be found in the family's records for this period, but these are nevertheless significant. We learn from them, for instance, that Sampson Lennard had installed some second cousins there – the first certain evidence that before the end of the 16th century members of the family were now living at Bayley. Shortly afterwards he and his wife applied to James I for permission to enclose 600 acres of land there, and also to create a park.[12]

The King duly granted the licence on 21 May 1610 in the following terms:[13]

> 'Since our beloved and faithful Samson Lennard of Hurstmonceux in our county of Sussex and Lady Margaret Dacre his wife have humbly prayed us that of our prorogative we would vouchsafe to grant them licence to erect a park with a free warren therein for deer the feeding and keeping of other wild beasts in the parish of Heathfield in the said county Know therefore that we, etc., have given, conceded, etc., to Samson Lennard Lord Dacre his wife their heirs etc full licence etc the power and authority to erect at his will a Park in Heathfield aforesaid as requested and to enclose, etc.,with pales ditch walls hedges 600 acres of pasture land with its woodlands part of which is now called Baylee'.

Some sources suggest that there had been an earlier medieval park at Heathfield, and it is possible that the Dacre's request was in part a move to legalise what already existed. On the other hand, many deer parks were destroyed during the Civil War, and it may have been a new creation. At all events, this development both consolidated the control of Lady Dacre and her husband over the estate at Heathfield, and its precious natural resources, and at the same time developed the parkland which has subsequently become so characteristic and prized a feature of the site.[14]

The exact location and size of the park at this time are uncertain: there are traces of a surrounding hedge and ditch both within the present wall and also well beyond it, for instance on land to the north of Cade Street. But the deer park did not necessarily extend over the whole area – and it also probably fluctuated in size at different periods. At all events, there is firm evidence for its existence in 1622, for in that year a group of seven local poachers was caught and subsequently brought before the Star Chamber by Lord Dacre. Among them were two members of a family which is still well-known in Heathfield – John and Robert Haffenden, the first described as a yeoman of Brightling. With them were one of his husbandmen, Richard Eggleston, and his servant William Herne, together with Richard Rabbett, Henry Martin and George Markwick. In reply to the accusation of having hunted deer in Bayley Park in March and April, John Haffenden claimed that he was invited by the keeper of the park, Francis Lennard (who owed him £27) and that in any case he had asked permission from Sir Francis Barnham who was in charge of the park in the absence of Lord Dacre.[15]

Another reference to the Park is found in John Evelyn's book *Sylva* ('A discourse of forest trees and the propagation of timber') published in 1664. By then it must have acquired a certain renown, for Evelyn wrote: 'The Rt.Honourable My Ld Dacres, as I am reliably informed, has a Park somewhere in Sussex almost environed with a hedge of Holly, able to keep in any game'. Although there was no specific mention of Bayley, this was certainly the park to which he was referring, as well as the hedge which was later reputed to be so compact that 'the smallest game could not escape from it'.[16]

THE LATER DACRES

Lady Margaret Dacre lived to be 70 and her husband, who died three years later in 1615, to 71. Their immediate successor, Henry Lennard, fell victim after one year to an epidemic, and his eldest son Richard who succeeded him devoted his energies to Chevening. Bayley in the meantime was occupied by another branch of the family. Heathfield Parish Register records the baptism of three children of Francis Lennard and his wife Judith: Philadelphia on 3 June 1619, Catherine on 16 April 1622, and a son, Francis, barely a year later, on 22 May 1623. Catherine lived for only just over a year: she died on 9 August 1623 and was buried at Heathfield Church, commemorated by a brass plate bearing an inscription and the Lennard arms. Another member of the family, Thomas Lennard, is also recorded in the parish register as having lost an infant child on 20 March 1617, though another – also called Thomas – was baptised on 4 June 1628.[17]

In 1630 Richard Lennard, Lord Dacre, died. In his will there was an explicit reference to 'Baylee' in the lands he bequeathed to his son Francis who was only 11 years old when he inherited. Four years later Francis also inherited extensive lands in Cumberland from the other branch of the family. But his title to them was contested, and the matter was only settled in the 1650s after many expensive years of litigation. In the meantime this Lord Dacre had a rather unhappy marriage – his wife found living in the country, which he preferred, dreadfully monotonous. She was also more of a Royalist then he: like many other important figures in Sussex he 'sided mostly with the Parliament' but after the civil war was able to obtain a royal pardon. He was less successful, however, in ordering his financial affairs: on his death in 1662 he left debts of £18,000. [18]

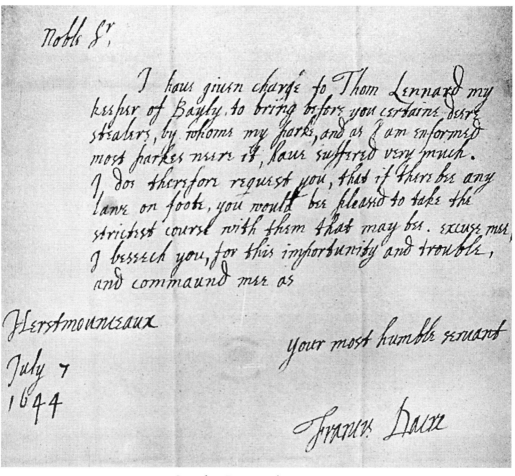

Letter from Francis, Lord Dacre 1644

Francis, Lord Dacre and his wife

During the lifetime of Francis Dacre, it was his brother who was keeper of the park at Bayley. He also had trouble with poachers, as is clear from this letter of 7 July 1644 from Dacre to Sir Thomas Pelham:[19]

'Noble Sr

I have giuen charge to Thom Lennard my keeper of Bayly to bring before you certain deere stealers, by whome my parke, and as I am enformed most parkes neere it, haue suffered very much. I doe therefore request you, that if there bee any lawe on foote, you would be pleased to take the strictest course with them that may bee. Excuse mee, I beseech you, for this importunity and trouble, and command mee as

Your most humble servant

FRANCIS DACRE'

This is probably the same person who is referred to in a Dacre account book dating from the 1640s which records that among Francis Dacre's guests at Herstmonceux castle there was 'Mr Lennard of Bayley, his kinsman'. The same source also mentions that in 1649 an annuity was being paid to 'Mr

Thomas Dacre, Earl of Sussex

Francis Lennard's widow', who may also have lived there at some stage. But the house may also have been rented out for some periods: there is, for instance, a reference to some of the Earl of Huntingdon's family living at Bayley, and in particular to the Rt.Hon Lord Hastings being there in September 1661.[20]

Francis Dacre died in 1662, leaving the estate to his son Thomas, who was only eight years old. Like his father, he became a student at Oxford a few years later but then – perhaps as a result of his mother's influence – was caught up with the court of Charles II. Ultimately this was to prove quite disastrous both for him and for the fortunes of the family. But initially he basked in the warmth of the monarch's favours. In the summer of 1674 at the age of twenty he married Lady Anne Fitzroy, the King's illegitimate daughter by Lady Castlemain, who later became Barbara, Duchess of Cleveland. This marriage gained for him the specially created title of Earl of Sussex, his appointment as a Gentleman of the Bedchamber, and the promise of a dowry of £20,000.[21]

But it proved to be a poor deal. The dowry was never paid; his wife soon showed a marked preference for the licentious pleasures of the court rather than living in the country and eventually went off to live in Paris with her mother, while Thomas sank ever deeper into debt. Part of the drain on his resources was accounted for by the alteration and modernisation of Herstmonceux Castle: but he also lost large sums gambling, and became involved in 'serious and expensive law suits' with some of his relatives. By 1692 he was in such trouble that he was obliged to petition Parliament for permission to sell some of his estates to pay off his debts. Chevening was rented out, and Herstmonceux sold in 1708.[22]

But long before that he had already disposed of Bayley Park: that was sold off on 18 January 1675 by Lord Dacre and Robert Lennard. It was the end of their families' involvement with Bayley, and the end of an era, for the man who bought it came from a very different background and brought with him a significantly different future for Bayley Park.[23]

A Country Seat (1675 - Today)

5. THE NEW OWNERS: LONDON MEN, AND THE FULLERS (1675–1766)

When Bayley Park was sold in January 1675 the country had entered a more settled period after the great turbulence of the Civil War. The ending of the Third Dutch War the previous year also ushered in fifteen years of peace between Britain and its European neighbours. Beyond that was to come the peaceful revolution of 1688 which ousted James II and brought William and Mary to the throne. And although there were to be many alarms about a Jacobite return until the middle of the 18th century, and another prolonged period of war with France, this was also a time of growing national prosperity. New wealth was being created, and those who acquired it sought the social symbols and status to go with it.

In Sussex one significant early sign of this was that between 1560 and 1640 at least twenty-five of the county's leading families substantially rebuilt their houses or built new ones. Many new deer parks were also created: already on the eve of the Civil War there were probably between seventy and a hundred of them in the county. By the seventeeth century 'no traveller through Sussex ...could fail to be impressed by the mansions and parks of the gentry'. It was not only the established local gentry who built. Already in the sixteenth century Sussex had become 'a favoured place of residence by parvenus and the most ambitious of the gentry', some of whom settled on lands put on the market after the dissolution of the monasteries.[1]

Part of the attraction of the county lay in its proximity to London, for although communications, especially in winter, were still difficult they had now begun to improve. Already by the end of the sixteenth century the cost of a coach had come within the means of many of the country gentry, and 'once Ashdown or the Horsham vale could be negotiated in a showy vehicle wives were keen to visit London'. Sir Thomas Pelham was one of the first in east Sussex to succumb to the attractions of life in the capital. From 1640 his stays there became longer: in December 1644 he spent Christmas there for the first time and subsequently he stayed in the capital each year from December to about May. The family 'spent the decade buying their way into fashionable London society'.[2]

But during the seventeeth century there was increasing movement in the reverse direction, too. Part of this was related to the growth of Tunbridge Wells as a fashionable spa town. The curative properties of its waters were discovered in 1606, and were patronised by Queen Henrietta Maria in 1630 when she was recovering from the birth of the future Charles II. Later that decade, in 1638, 'The Walks' were laid out as a promenade, and shops and houses also began to appear. After the disturbance of the Civil War and the rigours of the Commonwealth period, the Wells came into its own at the Restoration, when Charles II, his court and society frequented it during the season.

Celia Fiennes, a member of the same family that had owned Bayley, and one of several intrepid travellers it has produced over the centuries, visited the Wells in 1697 during the course of her travels around the country and gives a vivid picture of the town during the season. In addition to its Waters and its Walks there were several bowling greens for the Gentlemen, music for listening and dancing, several good Taverns ('all supply good wine'), Brew Houses for beer and Bakers for bread('But some of them come from London and spoyle the market by raising the price'). During the season, the Post came down from London every day except Monday and also went back every day except Saturday. It cost a 'penny Extraordinary' for a passenger to be brought the extra four miles from Tonbridge – then, as today, a 'post town' – though there were daily coaches from Tunbridge Wells to London for eight shillings a passenger during the whole of the season, and carriers twice a week.[3]

The availability of these services on a major route between east Sussex and the capital helped a good deal to make the area more accessible, and to offset the continuing difficulties of getting about the Weald during the winter months. Celia Fiennes called it 'a pleasant place to ride in in the summer and dry weather but a sad deep impassable road when much raine has fallen'. There was also the growing social allure of an area where, as she observed, 'there are several good houses all about'. These factors undoubtedly help to explain why Bayley was to prove tempting to London-based men of money when it came on the market in 1674.[4]

For these men such social considerations were probably of much greater importance than interest in local Wealden industry. In any case, this had begun a decline at the end of the 16th century which continued through and beyond the Civil War. Between 1574 and 1653, for instance, the number of furnaces in the county fell from 52 to 36, and the number of forges from 58 to 45. In the following fourteen years a further 22 furnaces and 24 forges went out of production. But the Heathfield area was an exception. Like some other parts of the Weald it concentrated on the production of castings rather than pig iron, and this provided the basis for a flourishing armaments industry. It specialised in the production of cannon and other ordnance, for which it maintained a reputation for excellence and had few serious rivals well into the middle of the 18th century. Fourteen furnaces and about the same number of forges were still operating in the Weald during this period.[5]

CONTENDERS FOR THE PARK

On 18 January 1675 Bayley was sold to Hercules Pawlett of Crookham in Crondall, Hampshire, a son of Sir Hercules Pawlett and grandson of the first Marquis of Winchester. He paid £1200 for the estate which then consisted of the park itself which extended to 117 acres, together with two coppices, several woods and fields and two 'house plots' which all together amounted to about another 125 acres.[6]

Pawlett remains a shadowy figure: it seems likely that he was no more than a middleman, who was used by Dacre and Lennard as a way of raising some much-needed ready cash, but who had no intention of holding on to the property himself. At all events there was also local interest in the estate. This came from the Ashburnham family. They had gone through a bad time during the

Ashburnham Place

period of the Commonwealth, the head of the family, Sir John Ashburnham (John the Cavalier) having been closely identified with Charles I. But with the Restoration their fortunes had recovered, and John and his brother William rebuilt Ashburnham Place and set about improving the estate.

Sir John Ashburnham died in 1671: it was his brother who showed an interest in Bayley. This is reflected in a series of letters to his godson, John Plummer, who was Steward at Ashburnham. At first, having heard of Pawlett's successful bid he feigned indifference, writing on 13 January 1675: 'As for Bayley Park lett it go we have lost nothing by itt, but what we never had'. But later he began to show much greater interest:[7]

> 'Ryde over one morninge very erly with my nephew and let him view it well and thinck thoroughly of itt, for though I am desiros of it and therefore will give the 1300 for itt, which is more by far than itt is worth, yett if he lyke it not very well theres an end of itt, for tis for him that I doe itt'.

The report was clearly positive, for on 16 March Ashburnham wrote:

> 'As for the business of Bayly Parke, I have a very great mynde to itt, but Pawlett has never come atte me since, nor indeed I thinck will not any more and I thinck it not best to send for him'.

He therefore suggested to his godson that he should signal his own continued interest in Bayley, saying that he wished an agreement could have been reached as he had a friend he hoped Ashburnham would appoint as his keeper there. By this indirect route he hoped to persuade Pawlett to reopen negotiations.

Initially the tactic seems to have worked, to judge by a letter dated 30 March in which Ashburnham wrote to his godson 'Conclude for Bayly Parke if you can'. But no deal was struck, and the next we hear of the matter – on 22 August that year – a man called Plummer (not apparently a relative of his godson) is trying to raise the cash to buy the Park. An intermediary who asked if Ashburnham would be willing to lend Plummer £100, was given a dusty reply: 'I answered not one penny, he said I should at his request give fifty, but I said I would not, and so we parted'. Ashburnham then reiterated his own interest in buying it:

> 'I thinck if the same gentleman (whom you know) should come againe to me and tell me that he had agreed for it for fifty Gynny more than the 1300 and the bargen in all things just as it was to have byn to me at first. I protest I so much doubt myself that I thinck I should give it. But truly I doe not thinck heel come

againe, for I am tould this morninge that he's gone today into his owne cuntry'.

So once more Ashburnham was frustrated, and there was worse to come. On 28 June the following year (1676) he wrote with some bitterness to his godson:

'Well now I see we may cast our [hat ?] for ever att Bayley Park which I am very sorry for and indeed if you had not byn too back-ward in it wee had not mist it but lett it now be forever and ever forgotten...Certaynely it is this fello of yor name that has gott the Park, and he lyke a knave did but fish you about it, for when he had once gott out of you that I would give 1300 l. for it he knew att worst he could be no looser by itt and went and bought it'.

In fact, for reasons which are not clear but may have been related to the conditions which Ashburnham sought to impose on the purchase, the property changed hands on 23 June 1676 for £1264, a good deal less than he had been prepared to pay. In addition to 'all that park called Baylee Park' of just over 117 acres, the estate then included two coppices (80 acres), Church Fields (18 acres), the Great, Little and Upper Meadows (7 acres), two Bramble Fields (10 acres), and various other small pieces of land, together with houses, a cottage, outhouses and commons – in total about 250 acres.[8]

JAMES PLUMMER: THE NEW MANSION

James Plummer was the new owner. He almost certainly had some local connections but was at the same time one of the new breed of entrepreneurs who had made money in the capital. He described himself as 'a citizen of London' and was a member of the Worshipful Company of Painters and Stainers - though the records of the Company, of which he became the youngest Warden in October 1676, testify to what has been described as 'his not very creditable civic career'. On several occasions he was fined for failure to attend meetings, to make due payments, and on his election as Warden, his refusal 'to give security for the stock of the Company as hath beene customary time out of minde'. He was clearly a very ambitious man, accustomed to sailing close to the wind, and was now determined to set himself up with a country seat worthy of his aspirations.[9]

Just over a year after his purchase of Bayley, on 3 August 1677, Plummer laid the first stone of a new house on the site.

Foundation stone of new mansion

There is documentary evidence that the building had been erected by 1682, and the painting attributed to the Dutch painter Gerard van Edema is probably a contemporary view of it *(see colour section)*. It was a substantial and imposing building, built mainly of brick, and designed in the new classical style which was quite different from the traditional iron masters' houses in Sussex with their steeply-sloping roofs, small windows, dark interiors and inglenook fireplaces. This was a modern mansion, with a sober rectangular exterior, its austerity relieved by large vertical windows, a portico running the length of its south-facing front, and two sculptured figures between the windows on the first floor. At either side of the main building there were also two detached pavilions.[10]

It was a fine example of a Restoration period mansion, and although it has subsequently been altered on many occasions, both inside and out – its present external appearance is largely due to changes made in the early part of this century by Sir Richard Blomfield – it still clearly bears the firm imprint of Plummer's original house.

As far as the immediate surroundings of the mansion are concerned we cannot unfortunately rely very much on van Edema. In the foreground he depicts a stylised scene of animals and rural pursuits, including two nude female bathers, and this element of fantasy is reinforced by the deer apparently roaming at will in a formal garden which leads up to the mansion itself. The suggestion that there was such a garden however, with one or more terraces leading down to the park, tends to be supported by the current configuration of the lawns on that side of the house.

Building the mansion involved a huge financial outlay which was ultimately to ruin both Plummer and his family. Some details of the massive borrowings he contracted have now come to light: they show a lengthening list of loans from John Turvin, a London haberdasher, which grew from an initial £1000 mortgage on property in London taken out in February 1673 before the purchase of Bayley Park to a massive debt of £4278.12s2d by November 1689. Plummer had already been forced to surrender to Turvin a property he had mortgaged in Kingston; now judgement was given against him in Chancery and he was ordered to pay his outstanding debts.

Fortunately for Plummer, Turvin then died – and without having made a will. This appears to have given Plummer some relief from his mounting financial problems. We lack evidence of how he managed to keep afloat in the following years, though there are hints that other 'citizens of London' may have come to his rescue. At all events, he was able to hold on to Bayley Park until his death seventeen years later.

But shortly after Plummer's death his elder son Charles was forced in October 1706 to transfer everything his father had possessed to Turvin's widow, Frances, to expunge his accumulated debts. The family was ruined. His own widow, Elizabeth, was able to save only a few trinkets, and his immediate offspring are reported to have 'sunk into pauperism'. Two of his daughters may however have fared rather better: they had married into local families – which suggests that the Plummers had been able for at least some time to enjoy the Park and live in the house of their father's dreams before it turned into a nightmare for them all.[11]

THE FULLER CONNECTION

Two years later, in June 1708, the Fullers stepped in to profit from the disaster. Bayley Park was then bought from Frances Turvin for a modest £900 by John Fuller of Tanners Manor, Waldron. This member of the family is generally known as 'Major John Fuller of the Trained Bands' to distinguish him from many other John Fullers of the same family. His purchase was the beginning of a connection between the Park and a notable local family which extended over several decades but which was to be curiously inconclusive:

Tanners Manor

43

characteristically the Fullers made use of the natural resources of the Park but never fully committed themselves to it.[12]

One reason for this may have been the heavy expenditure which the park and its house would have involved. But another no doubt was the fact that the family was already well established at Tanners Manor in Waldron. It was Major Fuller's great grandfather, described as a son of a 'citizen of London' who in 1575 bought the unexpired portion of the lease of Tanners. Since then the family had continued to make its mark locally by a combination of ambition, hard work and entrepreneurial skill - together with a prudent eye for the main chance which included a succession of judicious marriages.

Over the years the Fullers bought up land in and around Waldron as well as further afield. They both farmed themselves and let out land to tenants-at-will favouring the creation of bigger farms and experimentation with new crops and methods. But they also soon became heavily involved in the local iron industry. Initially they supplied fuel and iron ore for furnaces owned by others, like that of the Pelhams at Waldron, but in 1650 Captain John Fuller, grandson of the first Fuller to live at Tanners, went into partnership with Sir Thomas Dyke of Horeham (now Horam) to take a lease of Stream furnace and forge at Chiddingly for seven years so becoming an ironmaster in his own right.[13]

By this time Wealden production of pig-iron was in decline, and the Fullers were wise enough to concentrate on castings and, increasingly, on the production of ordnance. Having established a reputation for high-quality guns - their products were reckoned among the best the country produced - they were able to continue to flourish long after the rest of the industry had gone into decline. This explains why as late as 1693 the John Fuller who later bought Bayley Park built the New Furnace at Heathfield, one of only three to be constructed at that time. Located about a mile south of Heathfield parish church, on the left of the road to Vines Cross by Nettlesworth bridge, it was casting ordnance in quantity in the early years of the 18th century, and employing nearly half the population of Heathfield.[14]

Bayley Park occupied a strategic position up-stream from the Furnace where a number of springs were located and where water could be collected in holding ('pen') ponds ready for use when needed. Although it is not known precisely when those in the Park were constructed, it was almost certainly at this time: William Figg's map of 1819 shows five of them. According to one account they formed part of a continuing chain three miles in length containing eleven ponds in all. Even so they were not sufficient to enable the furnace to function throughout the year: its operations were largely confined to the winter months, and sometimes had to be curtailed as early as April.[15]

The most important customer for Fuller's guns was the Crown, through its Office of Ordnance: by the middle of the 18th century this aspect of the Fullers' activities could not have survived, in the face of the increasing competition from the Midlands, without the orders it placed. The guns had to be transported to Woolwich for trials and approval: this involved a difficult and expensive overland journey either to Lewes and Newhaven, from where they went by sea, or to Maidstone or another point on the Medway. Part of the Fuller's production also went either to Ireland or much further afield, including Italy: some of his cannon also eventually found their way to India.[16]

We do not know who lived at the Park during Fuller's thirteen years of ownership. He may well have continued to live at Tanners at Waldron, the freehold of which the family had acquired in 1617, with his wife Elizabeth Fowle (the daughter of another ironmaking family) and their four children. Any long-term interest they may have had in Bayley as a residence was certainly reduced by the purchase and rebuilding by his brother Thomas of the old mansion house at Brightling. In 1705 he gave this to John's eldest son (another John) who two years earlier had again greatly increased – as well as diversified – the family's fortunes by his marriage to Elizabeth Rose, daughter of Fulk Rose a wealthy planter and Governor of Jamaica. In honour of his wife, the Brightling house was then renamed Rose Hill. It was this house which was now to become the principal seat of the main branch of the Fuller family, where Major John's son fathered ten children and added political clout to the family's growing economic and social importance by his election in 1713 as a Tory Member of Parliament for Sussex.

Bayley Park was sold by Major John Fuller in December 1721. He made a characteristically good deal. The price was £2400 for 'the capital messuage or mansion house built by James Plummer', the Park and the surrounding estate – in all just over 227 acres – slightly less in extent than Fuller's original purchase for which he had paid £900. But Fuller still contrived to safeguard the all-important rights to its water in a covenant under which he reserved the liberty to draw water from the several ponds belonging to the premises 'as high as and including the Banqueting House pond' for the use of his furnaces, as long as the level did not go lower than 'the sluices laid for that purpose'.[17]

This must have been one of the last deals struck by the redoubtable Major Fuller, for he died the following year in May 1722. It was to be the end of the Fuller's ownership of Bayley Park, but not their connection with it, which was to be renewed in due course by his great-grandson.

RAYMOND BLACKMORE:
'A GENTLEMAN'S SEAT'

The incoming owner was another successful London businessman, a wine-merchant and a member of the Inner Temple. Like Plummer before him, Raymond Blackmore was in search of a country seat and the social status that went with it. According to the *Heathfield Memorials* he set about refurbishing the house and made it into 'a noble edifice built after the Corinthian order ...richly adorned with sculptured figures of sea and other animals'. It is not clear, however, how extensively Blackmore altered Plummer's original building, nor what Lucas means when he says he 'nearly completed' the house.[18]

Blackmore Raymnd Esq.r of Bailey.

Blackmore was to spend just over twenty years at Bayley. He made certain at an early stage that his arrival among the nobles and gentry of Sussex was properly recorded. Shortly after his purchase he became a subscriber to Richard Budgen's project to make a new map of Sussex. When it was published in 1724 he had the satisfaction of seeing both 'Baily' and 'Baily Park' clearly shown on it among the other 'Gentlemen's Seats' and his name and coat of arms displayed in the top row alongside those of other owners. And if at that stage he was very much a newcomer, by 1732 he had become sufficiently accepted to serve a term as High Sheriff of the county.

This may have had something to do with his ability to walk carefully where politics were concerned. In the parliamentary election of May 1734 his support was solicited both by Henry Pelham, brother of the Duke of Newcastle, and a Whig grandee, and also by Thomas Fuller, the local Tory candidate. Though himself a Tory, Blackmore chose to abstain. As Richard Burnett, the Duke of Newcastle's electoral agent in Heathfield reported:[19]

> 'I am told my Letter to Mr Blackmore ye Day before the Election
> kep him att home though he had promised Mr Fuller to go with
> him & he cald on him accordingly'.

But if Blackmore was prudent in politics, his social ambitions placed an increasing strain on his finances. Like Plummer before him, he contracted larger and larger loans to keep himself afloat. In February 1739 he had to take out an additional mortgage of £500, bringing the total to £1260: this was funded by Sir John Lade Bt, a member of the Warbleton family who made a fortune out of brewing. The situation must then have deteriorated further, for on 17 November the following year John Fuller, who was acting as a trustee for Sir John's estate, reported :[20]

'Mr Blackmore is down at Bayly, and I believe in very great distress for money he has sold a Bullock Lodge which he had sett up, but not Thatched, and is sellin of wood in the Park.

A Person came to me to know whither I would give leave to fell it (ie., wood in the Park)I told him if he paid the Interest I believed he might do it, but unless that was done, I believe it might be stoped from being carryed off, if not from being felled for it is a very bare Security for the Interest of £1200 besides the House which I believe no body will hire, the Plain Land will not lett for above £40 per annum or so much when the wood is off. I think Mr Calverly should be acquainted with this to putt a Stop to it, unless the Interest were paid, which I do not expect'.

By this time Blackmore must have been in poor physical as well as financial condition: he made his will in London on 26 April 1740 leaving everything to his wife and cutting off his brothers John and Henry with a shilling each 'in consideration of their extraordinary ingratitude towards me'. But within less than twelve months it was his brothers who were having to deal with his affairs, his wife having died before him and there being no children to succeed him. On 25/6 February 1742 they sold the property to another man from London.[21]

THE O'KEEFFES

The new owner, Arthur O'Keeffe, belonged to the same world of successful and ambitious professional men from the capital – but was nevertheless a rather surprising arrival at the Park. As far as we know, neither he nor his wife had any previous connections with Sussex: perhaps, like others, both before and since, they just chanced on Bayley Park at a time when they were looking for a country place.

Like his father before him, O'Keeffe was a barrister, having been admitted to Lincoln's Inn in 1738 and Gray's Inn in 1740. The family claimed descent from the Kings of Ireland, and had settled at Ballymaguirk in County Cork. Some of the family had supported the exiled Stuarts – one was killed at the battle of Aughrim in 1690 fighting for the deposed James II, and his three sons then fled and settled in France. But O'Keeffe's father, while he may have fought for Charles I, subsequently moved to London where he was admitted to Gray's Inn in 1682–3.[22]

On 4 April 1738 Arthur O'Keeffe married a wealthy widow, Isabella Casburne, who had a house in Piccadilly. Four years later he bought Bayley

Monument to O'Keeffe in Westminster Abbey

Park. At that time the estate appears to have been divided between the Blackmore brothers, Henry and John. From the former O'Keeffe bought the mansion, park, and surrounding land, totalling some 230 acres. For this he paid £2700, of which £2173.16s9d was paid to Henry Blackmore and £526.3s3d to Henry Barnes, to liquidate an outstanding debt contracted by Blackmore. From John Blackmore he purchased another 200 acres of wood, 60 acres of meadow, 50 acres of land, 50 acres of pasture, 40 acres of 'Furze and Heath and Common of Pasture for all maner of Cattle' as well as two messuages, four gardens and two acres of hop ground.[23]

As O'Keeffe was a practising barrister, it is likely that he and his wife lived only intermittently at the Park, using it as an occasional country retreat. But they must have taken up residence there at least for some time quite soon after their purchase, for he promptly sent his compliments to John Fuller who then called on them. It was also from Bayley Park that he wrote on 28 February 1745 to his new neighbour, Thomas Pelham, asking for modest preferment – a place on the Board of Commissioners for regulating hackney coaches 'which places were usually given to gentlemen at the Bar'. (O'Keeffe did not need to add that such places were also much sought after and very remunerative).[24]

When O'Keeffe died in 1756 the estate was inherited by his wife. As a London resident he chose to be buried in the cloister of Westminster Abbey where both he and his wife are recorded by an imposing memorial surmounted by a sculpted bust in the West Walk. The inscription recalls that he was descended from the Kings of Ireland, and that he was:

> 'The best of Husbands and the worthiest of Men.
> Deceit and guile he knew not:
> Honesty was an innate principle in him.
> He is gone to receive the Reward of
> A Virtuous and well spent Life'

This eulogy, characteristic of the times, seems nevertheless to have been an accurate reflection of his widow's sentiments. In a codicil to her will she asked that she should be recorded as 'his sincere friend and most affectionate wife', and added 'put my dear love's letters in a bag under my head in my coffin, and put mine to him under my feet'. She died six years later, at the age of 70, on exactly the same day - September 26 – as her husband.[25]

The park and its estate then passed, in the absence of a direct heir, to Arthur O'Keeffe's sister. But she had land elsewhere, in East Anglia, and had no interest in keeping Bayley Park. So in July 1766 it was sold yet again - this time to a man who was to become the Park's most famous owner. [26]

General George Eliott by Joshua Reynolds

6. THE WAR HERO: GENERAL GEORGE ELIOTT (1766-1790)

The new owner of Bayley Park was very different from his predecessors. Lieutenant General George Augustus Eliott was a military engineer, and a favourite of George II, who was to achieve great popular and national fame as 'Cock of the Rock' for his successful defence of Gibraltar during the prolonged siege of 1779-83. For this he was awarded the Order of the Bath, and later elevated to the peerage, taking the title of Lord Heathfield. His courage and determination were celebrated in widely-read accounts of the siege, in poems, and in paintings and prints - including a well-known portrait by Joshua Reynolds in the National Gallery.

Eliott's fame persisted for long after his death. An account of the siege by one of his officers, Captain John Drinkwater, first published in 1785 rapidly went into three editions, and was republished in 1844 and again in 1905. Writing in 1910, Perceval Lucas was still able to say of Eliott that 'his achievements are too well known to need recapitulation'. But since the end of Empire his achievement as Governor has receded and is now rarely recalled, even though he more than anyone else is responsible for Gibraltar having remained a British possession to this day. In the meantime a more complex story of the siege has also come to light since the first patriotic accounts of it were written. This does not however in any way diminish Eliott's achievement: he remains an outstanding figure who deserves to be remembered both locally and nationally.[1]

EARLY MILITARY CAREER

Eliott was a Scot, born on Christmas Day 1717, the seventh son of Sir George and Lady Eleanor Eliott of Wells House near Stobbs Castle Roxburghshire - a long-established border family. He needed to find his own way in the world, and decided at an early age to make the army his career. It was a good time to do so for Parliament and the country had at last, if reluctantly, begun to accept the need for a regular professional force. Throughout the seventeeth century Parliament had resisted the attempts of the Stuarts to create a permanent army under the monarch's direct control. It had been argued, with good reason, that the navy was the country's best form of defence and that a standing army at the disposal of the king would be a permanent danger to liberty.

During the eighteenth century, however, the situation changed. In the first place there was for many years a continuing threat from the exiled Stuarts and their allies at home and abroad. On the continent, Britain's Dutch and Hanoverian monarchs also needed British troops to defend their mainland possessions, and in particular to keep the French and the Spanish at bay. As the century wore on, these rivalries were more and more projected on to a much wider stage, as European countries sought to defend and extend their overseas empires – and none more vigorously than Britain itself, in America, in Canada, the West Indies, Africa and India. So there were plenty of wars to fight, and professional soldiers were needed to fight them.

The pattern of Eliott's education and his first steps towards a military career suggest that a good deal of care went into planning them, and that they were designed to give him access to, and experience of, the best professional military practice on the continent. After being privately educated, Eliott went to university at Edinburgh and Leiden, becoming fluent in French and German. He then attended one of the most prestigious of the French military academies at La Fère, in Picardy, which had been founded by Vauban. Following this, when still only seventeen, he joined the 23rd Foot and served during 1735–36 as a volunteer with the Prussian army, then a model for the rest of Europe. Returning home, he decided to train as a field engineer at Woolwich. At that time military engineers were part of the civilian Ordnance Office (they did not become part of the army until 1787) so having qualified, Eliott bought a commission in the 2nd Grenadier Horse Guards, then commanded by an uncle. No doubt benefiting from his patronage, he speedily rose from cornet to Lieutenant, and was appointed adjutant.

Eliott served with this regiment throughout the War of the Austrian Succession from 1742 to 1748 when on the death of Emperor Charles VI France, Spain, and Prussia combined to seek the break-up of the Austrian Empire. Britain, though already at war with Spain about trade privileges in Latin America (the so-called 'War of Jenkin's Ear') at first stayed neutral but the King was persuaded to side with Austria, and British troops were sent to the continent to help fight the French. At the battle of Dettingen in 1743, the last at which a British monarch personally led his army in the field, Eliott was wounded in an engagement during which the British only just escaped encirclement by the French. But he also had a stroke of luck: although only a very junior officer, he attracted the favourable attention of George II, who was later to appoint him as his aide-de-camp.

This was at the beginning of the Seven Years' War in 1756, by which time Eliott had purchased his way to the rank of Lieutenant Colonel. The conflict was a continuation of the struggle with France, now allied with Austria, and was not only about predominance in Europe but also, and increasingly, a colonial war for territory in America, Canada, India and the West Indies. Eliott's part in it, however, was initially on the continent. After three years on his staff, George II commissioned him to raise a regiment of light horse on the Prussian model, the first of its kind in the British army, which later became the 15th Light Dragoons and then the 15th Hussars. As Colonel of the new regiment Eliott distinguished himself in campaigns in Germany during 1759–1761 alongside the army in which he had earlier served. He earned the repeated thanks of Prince Ferdinand of Prussia for his contribution, which included a successful engagement at Emsdorf when his regiment captured five battalions of French infantry complete with their colours and nine guns.

Promoted Major-General in June 1759 Eliott was placed in charge of the cavalry in an attack on the French coast in 1761, and the following year had the good fortune to become second in command to the Earl of Albermarle on an expedition to seize Cuba, in response to Spain having entered the war. This involved the successful siege and capture of Havana the following year, in an operation in which views on Eliott's part differ sharply. While one source claimed that he was 'conspicuous by his valour and constancy', a recent account is more sceptical, claiming that he was barely mentioned in the accounts of the siege. What is not in dispute, however, is that Eliott did very well financially out of the operation, his share of the prize money amounting to the huge sum of £24,539.10s 1d.[2]

It was with a modest part of his new fortune that Eliott bought Bayley Park three years later in July 1766. His interest in it was probably related to the local production of cannon. Fuller was an important supplier to the Board of Ordnance at Woolwich where he had to send his products for testing and approval. (His correspondence is full of the difficulties he had in transporting them there, and sometimes in getting them accepted). So during his spell of training as a field engineer, and also later as a gunner, Eliott would have become familiar with Heathfield and its armaments industry. As a man accustomed to the rigours of military life, he was clearly not put off by Horace Walpole's description in 1749 of the Sussex scene[3]:

> 'If you love good roads, good inns, plenty of postillions and
> horses, be so kind as never to go into Sussex. We thought
> ourselves in the northest part of England; the whole country has
> a Saxon air and the inhabitants as savage as if George the Second
> was the first monarch of the East Angles… Sussex is a great
> damper of curiosity'.

In the same year the Duke of Richmond complained about another aspect of life in Sussex. 'The common people of this country have no notion', he said, 'that smuggling is a crime'. He added that places in the Weald such as Hawkhurst and Goudhurst lived in an atmosphere of 'open defiance of all the laws and all government whatsoever'. But this did not greatly concern General Eliott either: he was accustomed to dealing with the rougher side of life.

PURCHASE OF BAYLEY PARK

Eliott was able to buy Bayley Park from Mary Anne O'Keeffe for £4000, although by then the estate had grown to some 800 acres. According to the sale particulars, it now consisted of '3 messuages, 4 gardens, 100 acres of land, 100 acres of meadow, 100 acres of pasture, 200 acres of wood, (and) 300 acres of Furze and Heath and Commons of pasture for all manner of Cattle'. So, together with its mansion, it offered a very decent country seat, in a very agreeable setting, at the centre of a gun-making area and at the same time not too far from London.[4]

It was also a suitable place for Eliott's family. In June 1748 he had married Anne Pollexfen, a Devonshire heiress, daughter of the last Sir Francis Henry Drake of Buckland Abbey. They had now a teenage son and a daughter. At the age of 48 Eliott was ready to combine his flourishing military career with that of a country gentleman.

He soon set about making the house to his liking. He enclosed some land in front of it to provide greater privacy, and employed one of the leading architects of the day, Robert Taylor, to completely gut and rebuild the interior. Taylor had begun his professional life as a sculptor, and only turned to architecture when he was forty. But his ascent was rapid, becoming Surveyor to the Bank of England in 1754, and later holding a series of other public offices for which he was knighted in 1782. The plans of the changes he made to the mansion in the Park have not so far come to light, but he probably inserted the Venetian window in the north facade and five bay windows at the western end. At all events, there is no reason to doubt the claim which was later made that the result was a 'capital and modern mansion…fitted up with great Neatness, Elegance and Convenience'.

During Eliott's period of ownership a riding school was also added, his son becoming an enthusiast of the *haute école* and a well-known breeder of horses. Eliott also substantially enlarged the estate, purchasing large areas of the common waste on Heathfield Down from the Sackville family, who owned it as part of the Manor of Heathfield. During the twenty-five years that Eliott

THE DUKE AND THE GENERAL

In January 1767 Eliott's arrival was welcomed by the Duke of Newcastle, who immediately solicited his support for his candidate in an impending parliamentary election:[5]

Sir,

As I have desired the Favor of the Gentlemen in my Neighbourhood in Sussex, to attend the election of my Lord George Lennox, on Tuesday next at Lewes, I hope you will excuse the Liberty I take, in desiring the same Favor of you.

As we now have the pleasure of having you Settled amongst us, I should be very glad, if I could be of any use to you, in making the County agreable to you. The Gentlemen of my Neighbourhood, and Myself, have one Favor to ask of you, That you would allow us, to have you put into the Commission of Peace, where you might be of great Service to the Country.

I beg pardon for giving you this Trouble; and am, with great Respect, Sir,

>   Your Most Obedient
>   Humble Servant,
>   Holles Newcastle

From his London address in Curson Street, Eliott replied on 29 January:

My Lord

I have the honour of your Grace's letter, and shall not fail to attend at the Election; tho' as yet I have not been long enough in the County to be properly introduc'd to your Grace, I esteem it a most distinguished favour, that you'll please to grant me your protection and countenance, but I fear 'twill be impossible for me to accept the very obliging offer of being in the Commission supposing me ever to be under a necessity of acting as My Lord you must be sensible that Camps are not the best School for a Magistrate.

I have the honour to be
>   With the greatest Respect
>   Your Grace's
>   Most Obedient
>   and most humble servant,
>   G.A.Eliott.

Two views of Baily Park c.1770
(From drawings by Samuel Hieronymus Grimm)

owned the park he added nearly 600 acres to those he had originally bought, bringing the total to just under 1400 acres: a sizeable estate for the Weald. Of these some 550 acres were directly managed, the remainder being let to tenants. Among the farms in this latter category - several of which are still there today - were Brailsham, Bingletts, Gamelands, Holebans, Hugletts, Kiln, Little Tottingforth (Tottingworth), Lucks, Mount Pleasant, Scudland, Siggs, Sky, and Store House.[6]

One of Eliott's more spectacular activities while at the Park was to experiment with red-hot shot. He wanted to find out the heat required to bring a hundredweight or so of iron to a cherry-red state, and how best to load the shot to avoid premature ignition of the charge. 'Accordingly', it is reported, 'the people of Heathfield, with some alarm, were to see their skies lit with incandescent balls that soared in great sparking arcs, followed by the crashing of timber and the breaking out of fires. The originator of this spectacle could be seen, ghoulishly lit by the glowing coals of an open grate, and surrounded by cats, to which he was addicted'. Whatever the people of Heathfield thought at the time, these experiments were later to be put to good use during Eliott's defence of Gibraltar.[7]

GEORGE GILBERT: 'THE APOSTLE OF SUSSEX'

The General's generosity to one of his former soldiers was also to have some unexpected consequences for the local community. After arriving at Bayley Park he was approached by George Gilbert, a local man born in Rotherfield, who had served with him during the Hanoverian wars in the 15th Light Dragoons. Eliott offered him a job and rapidly promoted him to become foreman on his staff at the Park. But Gilbert was no ordinary soldier: he had undergone a religious conversion and become an ardent Calvinistic Methodist. His preaching and evangelising activities soon aroused much hostility among a section of the local population which boiled up at a dinner which the General gave for his freeholders. They had decided to tell the General that they wanted him to get rid of Gilbert:[8]

> 'After dinner the General came in to see his guests, and when the person who was appointed to take the lead in this mean and contemptible business commenced a speech, concluding it with an earnest request that he would send him away, the General immediately rose from the table in anger, and exclaimed: 'Gilbert is a good soldier and a worthy fellow, and you shan't hurt him'. He then left the room, and their project failed'.

The Independent Chapel, Chapel Cross

Subsequently Mrs Eliott also intervened on Gilbert's behalf to get his discharge from the army. By then he had succeeded, in spite of continuing opposition, in raising £100 to build a chapel locally in 1769; as a former professional carpenter he made most of the pulpit himself. Such was the success of his ministry that in 1777 it was pulled down and replaced by a much larger one - the immediate forerunner of the present Independent Chapel at Chapel Cross which was erected in 1808. He became a full-time minister and an itinerant preacher, visiting some sixteen towns and villages in regular rotation, including Alfriston, Battle and Rotherfield where new chapels were built. He acquired great renown during the rest of a long life which lasted until 1827, when he died at the age of eighty-six. His long ministry drew on the local tradition of independence of thought and non-conformity, and provided a new focus for it which continues to be a feature of the religious life of Heathfield today.

THE GIBRALTAR INHERITANCE

Eliott's own career seems to have reached a plateau for a number of years until 1774, after which he spent little time at Bayley Park. His absence may have been in part due to the death of his wife in 1772, but it was also because the remainder of his military career took him out of the country. He was probably fortunate not to become involved in the war with the rebellious American colonies which broke out in 1774: in that year he was appointed Commander in Chief in Ireland. This was certainly an important post, given the increasing danger of revolt there too. But almost before he had time to unpack his bags Eliott found himself in conflict with the civil government, asked to be relieved of his post, and returned to England.

This was a serious setback, and could have been the end of his career as he was now nearing sixty. But in 1776 he was appointed Governor of Gibraltar, another hot spot, and it was there he was to achieve his greatest success. His training as a gunner must have been an important consideration in his appointment, and that fact that his uncle, Colonel Roger Eliott, had earlier occupied the same position no disadvantage. At all events, it was considered an important front-line post given that the Spanish were determined to recover this strategically-important rocky headland which commanded the entrance to the Mediterranean.

Gibraltar had been captured in August 1704 by the British during the War of the Spanish Succession by an expedition commanded by Admiral Rooke and Sir Cloudesley Shovell, and British sovereignty had been confirmed by the Treaty of Utrecht in 1713. George I and some of his ministers however considered it a liability, and five years later offered to return it to Spain if suitable compensation could be arranged. It cost £90,000 a year to garrison, its harbour was shallow and treacherous, and the place itself was hot, dirty, ruined and disease-ridden. The Spanish would allow no trade with it by land, and made it clear that there could be no peace with them unless and until it was returned. In 1727 they tried, unsuccessfully, to recapture it by force and two years later began to erect fortifications on the narrow isthmus leading to the Rock. Thirty years later, William Pitt the Elder tried again to arrange an exchange with the Spanish but no deal was struck and the issue remained unresolved.

Eliott was appointed to Gibraltar at a point when Britain was confronted with a very dangerous situation. Its American colonies were in rebellion, and Ireland was on the brink of revolt: the country was isolated and its armed forces in disrepair. In July 1776 the American colonies declared their independence and a series of scattered engagements developed into war. By the time Eliott arrived at Gibraltar in May 1777 this was already going badly, and worse was to follow. The surrender of Burgoyne's army at Saratoga in October that year was not only a major military disaster from the British point of view, but also brought France into the war the following year. Spain followed in 1779, allying itself with France in a secret convention which pledged the support of her fleet for an invasion of Britain that summer, in return for a French commitment to help Spain recover Gibraltar. On 21 June that year the siege and blockade of Gibraltar began: it was to last for three years, seven months and twelve days.

As the Rock was generally held to be impregnable from any attack across the narrow isthmus joining it to the land, sea power held the key to its capacity to survive. The Spanish clearly hoped initially that they could starve the Rock into submission: the build-up of their land-forces and artillery proceeded at a leisurely pace. But although they were able severely to restrict supplies, they were never able to impose a totally effective blockade. This was partly because of the inherent difficulties of doing so, given changing wind and other weather conditions, but also – and more crucially – because the British were able in spite of their stretched resources to mobilise sufficiently powerful fleets to ensure that supply convoys and reinforcements were able to get through from time to time. Nevertheless, the successful defence of Gibraltar also required effective and determined leadership on the part of its Governor. He had to ensure and maintain discipline and morale, to devise and carry out a strategy for its defence against attack by land or sea, and to maintain the vigilance of its garrison.

For these tasks General Eliott was well equipped. He was an experienced professional soldier, with a robust physical presence, and a man of austere habits in spite of his florid appearance, rarely eating meat or drinking wine or spirits. He was reputed never to sleep for more than four hours a night, and during the siege to have been the first up and the last to go to bed. He also had the reputation of a stern but just disciplinarian, and while some found him intractable and secretive, he was also known for his courteous and generous gestures. He was greatly respected, even if he did not often inspire warmth or affection.[9]

THE SIEGE BEGINS

In the two years before the siege began Eliott had taken urgent steps to reinforce its defences: as soon as news of the rupture with Spain arrived the garrison was put on alert. Eliott also rationed fresh meat and – with characteristic attention to detail – ordered his soldiers to stop powdering their hair in order to conserve stocks of white flour. But although the Spanish cut off communications by land and imposed a close blockade by sea from 18 July, they made no offensive move against the Rock. It was Eliott who ordered the first shots to be fired at 6.30am on Sunday morning 12 September 1779. This was partly to raise the spirits of the garrison and civilians on Gibraltar, where fresh provisions were beginning to be scarce, and partly as an act of defiance against the Spanish. Accounts of it vary widely: according to the one which gained popular credence Eliott invited the recently-wed wife of one of his officers to apply the lighted taper to the touch-hole of the cannon, and then, raising his hat and shaking it in the direction of Spain, shouted "Britons, strike home!"[10]

These were brave words, but the reality of the following months was increasingly grim. There were over 8000 people on the Rock to be fed: about 3000 civilians and a garrison of just under 5,400, consisting of six British and three Hanoverian regiments. In January 1780 Eliott reported that no vessels

Engraved for RAYMOND's History of England.

GENERAL ELLIOT haranguing his troops, previous to the ATTACK of the Gun Boats at GIBRALTER, September 13, 1782.

General Eliott and senior officers during the siege. Painting by G Carter.

had been able to get through, and that many of the civilian population were near starvation. But in the middle of that month a relief convoy arrived with supplies and reinforcements, escorted by a fleet commanded by Admiral Rodney. On its way to the Rock he had first chased and captured 22 Spanish vessels including a 64-gun ship and six other warships, and then fought a daring and very successful engagement against another Spanish force in a great storm on a lee shore and partly at night. In this the Spanish lost a 70-gun ship which blew up, and four other ships of the line taken as prizes.

The spirits of the garrison were temporarily raised but when the fleet sailed away on 13 February, it was watched in silence. Within a few weeks much of the flour it had brought was rotten, the pease magotty, and the meat stinking. The following month rations had to be reduced; many of the new troops fell sick; scurvy claimed its first victim; and a smallpox epidemic broke out. Eliott incurred much hostility from the wives of the garrison when he refused to inoculate the children, on the grounds that it could kill more than it saved from the disease. Some 500 wives and children are estimated to have died from the epidemic, in addition to several hundred soldiers, but fortunately for Eliott it was over by August.

In the meantime, on Wednesday 7 June, the Spanish launched a surprise attack by sea on the harbour, sending in six blazing hulks as fireships in an attempt to destroy the naval and other ships at anchor. These were a fearsome sight, described by one observer as 'moving mountains of fire'. But the wind dropped and boats from the garrison were able to grapple with the fireships and tow them away before they could do any appreciable damage. The hulks were later broken up and sold as much-needed firewood.

While desultory shelling continued, the garrison suffered far more during the following two years from the blockade and the weather. The prolonged fierce heat of the summer in 1780 was followed by a cold, wet winter: hunger, disease and boredom were rife. In February 1781 Eliott had to deal with a demand by his officers for higher pay to offset spiralling prices; and in March he had to reduce the bread ration for the troops still further. In early April another relief convoy under Admiral Darby arrived in the nick of time. But the same day the Spanish, for the first time, launched an intensive bombardment of the Rock from land and sea which destroyed much of the town. When troops were used in an attempt to control the widespread fires, they discovered stores of liquor and other goods which had been stashed away. Large-scale looting followed. 'Such a scene of drunkeness, debauchery and destruction was hardly ever seen before', wrote one officer. Eliott, for his part, reported on the 'scandalous irregularity' of the British regiments, adding that 'except Rapes and Murders there is no one crime but what they have been repeatedly guilty of'.[11]

From now on the bombardment was to become an almost daily feature of the siege, broken only by the regular Spanish post-lunch siesta. Its intensity varied, but in the first seven weeks it was particularly intense, some 77,000 shots being discharged. About half the civilian population took the opportunity to leave when Darby sailed away towards the end of April. But in spite of stern measures, it took some weeks to restore order among the garrison. A soldier caught in the act of looting was hanged at the beginning of May, and two more at the end of the month. Another was sentenced to a thousand lashes. In October there was a mutiny on the cutter Speedwell.

Eliott's response to the growing disaffection was to give his troops something to do. Very early on the morning of Sunday 26 November two thousand of them launched an attack on newly-constructed Spanish fortifications on the isthmus. It involved a considerable risk as almost a third of the garrison's total strength was committed to the operation - and Eliott compounded it by accompanying his men to see it for himself. But fortune favoured the brave. The raiders completely surprised their enemy, destroyed the batteries, and successfully completed their 'Grand Sally' by 5am, with only very light

TERROR to the DONS or the GOVERNOR–Instructing his LITTLE FAMILY.

casualties. It was a bold stroke which served an important psychological as well as useful military purpose, and was characteristic of the cool brain which Eliott concealed behind his bluff exterior.

PREPARING FOR THE GRAND ATTACK

As 1782 arrived, hard on the heels of the news of a British disaster in America at Yorktown, it promised to be a decisive year. Talk of peace was in the air: but so too were rumours of preparations for a decisive Franco-Spanish attack on the Rock. For several months it was not at all clear which was the more likely. The threat of starvation and disease now receded, with the arrival early in February of further supplies and a Portugese ship with a cargo of 30,000 oranges. Late in March more ships got through, including four transports carrying 700 men of the 97th Regiment – though many quickly fell sick and more than a hundred of them were to die within the next few months.

It was now the military and naval threat which was the major challenge. In February the Spanish captured Minorca, and the following month the build-up of their forces began. But this coincided with the fall of Lord North's government back home, and the opening of peace negotiations with the Americans, French and Spanish. Both George III and his ministers were anxious to do a deal over Gibraltar, the only problem being what compensation to seek for its return to Spain. Public opinion, on the other hand, was increasingly vociferous in favour of the Rock and its defenders. Caught between the devil and the deep blue sea, the government dithered. The foreign secretary sent a half-hearted message of support to Eliott:

> 'I send this to acquaint you of the measures we are taking to give
> you as early a Support as possible in Men, Provisions and Stores:
> They may reach you a little sooner or later, but you may be
> assured that the Relief is intended to be effectual'.

It was not however until 14 August that the Cabinet decided that the Fleet should be sent 'at latest in the first week of September with the Necessaries and Supplies for the relief of the Garrison of Gibraltar'. This meant that Eliott would have to fend for himself in the face of the Grand Attack expected early that month.[12]

Eliott was acutely aware that he now lacked close political allies at Court and in the British government: there were also tensions within the group of his senior officers. But these were trivial compared with the conflicts within the Franco-Spanish high command. In June the Duc de Crillon, a 64 year old French general, had taken over from General Alvarez. He was a man of great experience and military distinction. But he soon found himself in conflict over the conduct of the Great Attack with a brilliant 49 year-old French engineer, Michaud d'Arcon, who planned to deploy ten specially-built vessels as huge floating batteries with which to pound the Rock's defences from the sea. These were equipped with 142 large cannon, the decks being protected by roofs and 7-8ft thick walls of wet sand, cork and other materials, as well as a primitive sprinkling system designed to make them impregnable against red hot shot. The French commander did not think much of these new-fangled contraptions, nor did he properly coordinate his plans for the attack with the Spanish admiral Cordoba. But the size and strength of the naval and land forces under his command made him confident of success.

The Franco–Spanish force that had been assembled was one of the largest ever deployed for the siege of a single fortress. The Combined Fleet consisted of 44 line-of-battle ships and hundreds of smaller vessels, and the land force of 40,000 Spanish and French troops, supported by 200 heavy guns and mortars. Command of the sea seemed secure, for Eliott had only a few gunboats and other small vessels, and there was no sign of the British fleet. The garrison numbered barely 6000 weary men (most of whom had been on the Rock throughout the siege) supported by 100 cannons and mortars. In Paris the conquest of the Rock was already being celebrated in August with a theatrical piece which played to thunderous applause; in the middle of the month two French royal princes, the Comte d'Artois and the Duc de Bourbon, arrived to take part in the proceedings; and a crowd of spectators estimated at 80,000 gathered from all over Europe on the surrounding hills in anticipation of the expected triumphant assault.

The Duc de Crillon was anxious to launch the attack, but met with protests from d'Arcon that his 'flottantes' were not yet ready. The assault should have begun on Saturday 7 September but it was postponed until the following Friday. Eliott's men had been expecting the attack. When it failed to materialise the General decided, on the advice of his deputy, Lieutenant-General Robert Boyd, to launch a pre-emptive strike. A heavy cannonade was opened at 7am on the Sunday morning, and continued for the next nine hours: over 5000 shot were fired during that time at the Spanish positions on the isthmus. The Spanish replied, but their main redoubt in the centre of their line was silenced, and they suffered heavy casualties.

On the following day, Monday 9 September, the Spanish replied with a heavy barrage which began at daybreak and continued all day, a 64-gun battery

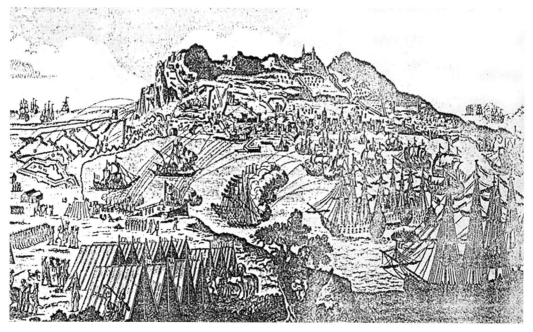

The Grand Attack

enfilading the British defences on the Rock and causing much damage. There was also a heavy bombardment from the sea. But Eliott's initiative had unsettled his opponents, and forced Crillon to show his hand before he was ready. It also made the French commander all the more determined to brook no further delay in spite of continuing arguments with his colleagues about timing and tactics. When the Grand Assault was finally launched it was in some confusion.

THE FINAL RECKONING

It was nevertheless a fearsome sight as the Combined Fleet under Admiral Don Luis de Cordoba sailed into the Bay on the morning of Thursday 12 September 1782, flying the flags of ten admirals. Together with the ships already there this made a force of 47 ships of the line, 8 frigates and a large number of smaller ships including 100 gunboats and 300 troop carriers. The main attack was to be from the sea on the western side of the Rock, where its natural defences were weaker than elsewhere, but had been supplemented by stout and heavily-armed fortifications. These had first to be pounded into submission: this was the task assigned to d'Arcon's floating batteries. When shortly before 7am on Friday 13 September these weighed anchor and began to sail towards the Rock, Eliott knew that the Grand Assault was about to begin. Although surprised to see them – he had thought they would only move at night time – he immediately gave orders for the fires to be lit to heat up the defenders' shot.

When the floating batteries were still over 2000 yards away, they turned east and formed a line of battle facing the Rock. A sandbank which d'Arcon had discovered only the previous evening prevented a number of them advancing much closer to the shore. Nevertheless it was an impressive sight when they opened fire, a heavy bombardment in which the land-based batteries also joined: 300 guns against the garrison's 100. Eliott's men were able at first to reply only with cold shot, and were amazed to see it bouncing off the roofs and walls of the 'flottantes'. But, because of the way the floating fortresses listed in the water, and the distance some of them had to remain from the shore, their fire was partially ineffective. Most of the casualties among the garrison were caused by the land-based batteries.

At last, at midday, the defenders' shot was glowing red, and Eliott ordered its use by the 39th and 72nd regiments. They maintained a furious rate of fire. But at first this also seemed to have no effect: the floating batteries appeared as impregnable as d'Arcon claimed. The hot sun was beating down, and many of the gunners were suffering from acute thirst. It was not until two in the afternoon that smoke began to rise from the nearest (and one of the largest) of the batteries, the *Talla Piedra*, and later that its fire began to slacken. Towards 5pm smoke began to pour from the bulkhead below its topdeck: for several hours a shot had lodged unseen, but fire now threatened a munition store. Firing ceased as its crew tried in vain to douse the flames: the battery was now crippled and immobile as its sails had been shot to ribbons. It signalled to the distant friendly shore for help, as did its neighbour, the flag-ship *Pastora*, where a number of fires had also broken out – but Crillon replied that the wind was in the wrong quarter. Gradually, as evening fell, the barrage from the floating batteries became more and more sporadic, and the land-based batteries fell silent, lacking both orders and ammunition, having fired nearly 40,000 rounds that day. By six o'clock that evening the Garrison sensed victory.

It was not until later that night, however, that the threat from the floating batteries was finally removed. At 1am the two nearest to the Rock suddenly exploded in flames, and two hours later four more were enveloped by fire. British gunboats set off from the Rock to finish them off and to rescue survivors, but they were withdrawn out of danger when at 5am another float-ing battery blew up, as did four more later in the morning, the final one about midday. Another burned down to water-level. The garrison claimed – and popular accounts of the siege repeated – that all the damage had been done by their red-hot shot. The truth was more complex. The nearest floating batteries had indeed been crippled by the defenders' guns. But when Crillon's appeal to the fleet to tow them to safety failed, he decided that they had to be destroyed to prevent them falling into the hands of the British. When the Combined Fleet eventually arrived at midnight, it was to evacuate their crews under cover of darkness as the floating batteries were set alight. But the operation went badly wrong, and many either perished in the flames or were drowned. It was in neither side's interest to trumpet the truth of what had really happened.

The failure of the Grand Assault was the crucial turning point in the siege, and Eliott was right to claim it as a famous victory for the garrison. In its wake the threatened land-based assault was called off. But this was by no means the end of the affair. Supremacy at sea had still to be re-established and the garri-son re-supplied: this was the task of the fleet under Howe which had belatedly left Spithead on 11 September and finally arrived at the entrance to the Straits of Gibraltar on 9 October. A major engagement with the Combined Franco-Spanish fleet was expected: Cordoba had 44 ships of the line to Howe's 34. But bad weather had wrecked havoc with the French and Spanish ships and prevented them engaging the British fleet before its arrival. So even though the convoy initially overshot the harbour, in the following days the 31

The Bombardment of Gibraltar ... Thunder.

Gibraltar

'Gainst Elliot the French & the Spaniards, Combin'd
Are throwing their Stink Pots you see from behind
That the Garrison's Safe you must own is no Wonder
For all that they do is but F—t—g at Thunder.

ordnance ships were shepherded safely in, and two regiments of reinforcements disembarked from naval vessels. Subsequently, although Howe was prepared for battle, there were only minor skirmishes before the combined fleet broke off the engagement and returned to port, leaving Howe to sail off unchallenged back home.

For another month the Spanish continued to fire five to six hundred rounds a day at the garrison, but from November their numbers on the ground decreased rapidly. Eliott, however, kept up his guard. Like other Scots, he took little notice of Christmas Day and he chose it to launch a raid on the Spanish positions. In January 1783 he also banned his officers from taking any further part in amateur theatricals with which they were now whiling away the time. On 2 February Crillon informed the Governor that the preliminaries of a general peace had been signed, and three days later the blockade was lifted. Rather characteristically, Eliott forbade any fraternisation with the Spanish troops until formal confirmation of the peace arrived from England, which it did finally on 10 March. But then full military courtesies were resumed. Eliott went out to meet and embrace the French commander, Crillon, and each subsequently took the other on a conducted tour of their fortifications.

Over the whole period of the siege the attacking forces lost 1473 men killed, wounded or missing, and another 357 taken prisoner. The Gibraltar garrison, for its part, had a similar number of casualties: 1729 were killed, died from wounds or sickness, or were disabled. In addition, it is estimated that some 500 soldiers' wives and children also died in the smallpox epidemic. Among the general public these losses, however much regretted, were of small account compared with the satisfaction derived from the successful defence of 'the Rock' in the face of apparently overwhelming odds. At a time when there was little good news for the country elsewhere, this elicited a powerful surge of patriotic feeling and widespread acclaim for Eliott himself, who rapidly became a popular hero. His exploits, and those of the garrison were celebrated in many patriotic accounts in prose and verse, as well as in paintings and prints. A typical example is that of a poem written by a soldier, which began:[13]

> 'At Eliott's name (which none conceal)
> Each Briton is delighted,
> And foreigners a pleasure feel,
> To hear his deeds recited'.

THE INCONVENIENT HERO

The King and Shelburne for their part, however, were greatly embarrassed by this surge of popular feeling. They wanted to get rid of Gibraltar, believing that its retention would prevent good relations with Spain, whom they were anxious to prize away from France. George III wanted to exchange it for islands in the West Indies, while his prime minister favoured Minorca and Florida. By December a preliminary agreement was reached with Spain over the compensation to be obtained for the return of Gibraltar, as part of a complex peace package including also America and France. So strong however was the opposition in Parliament and the country that this deal had rapidly to be abandoned. In return for keeping the Rock, Britain returned Minorca to Spain, which also gained all of Florida. For many the retention of Gibraltar was the only positive aspect of a settlement which was otherwise badly received, leading to Shelburne's fall from office early in 1783.

Eliott's popularity was therefore rather unwelcome to the King and his principal ministers. Under parliamentary pressure he was nevertheless given the Order of the Bath, and a pension for life of £1500 per annum. An attempt in

Baily Park, the seat of Lord Heathfield (1788)

parliament to raise this rather meagre sum was nevertheless successfully resisted. Eliott himself remained on the Rock, attending to the reorganisation of the garrison and the problems of those leaving the army. It was on 23 April 1783, St George's Day, that the victory was celebrated. Eliott paraded the garrison and formally gave them the thanks of the King and the country. 'No army', he said, 'has ever been rewarded by higher national honours. The nations of Europe are struck with admiration of your gallant behaviour'. General Boyd, acting on behalf of the King, then invested him with the red insignia of his new honour.[14]

It was another four years before Eliott returned to Britain, and only then, when he was 70, that he was raised to the peerage and took the title of Lord Heathfield. A pen portrait of him on his return by his nephew described him as 'a fine old man (who) preserves a sort of beauty which is his character and consists in tolerable freshness and features of a marked and commanding style'. He had 'a brisk, lively manner full of attention and civility', and was very bound up with his profession and with Gibraltar, where he intended to be buried.[15]

In this respect, however, he was to be frustrated. On 6 July 1790 he died of the palsy two days before he had intended to set off there from his residence near Aix-la-Chapelle. He was brought back to Heathfield and interred in a vault built in the chancel of the parish church for that purpose. But this was not to be his final resting place. Sometime later his remains, and those of his wife, were transferred to her family's burial place at Buckland Monachorum in Devon. It is in St Andrew's church there that an imposing monument to him is to be found in the Drake chapel, an outstanding example of the work of the 18th century sculptor John Bacon. There is also a fine full-length statue of him by Charles Rossi R.A. in St Paul's cathedral, 'erected at the public expense', if somewhat belatedly, in 1826.

DAUGHTER AND SON

During Eliott's absence in Gibraltar - and also after his return when he lived mainly in London - the family association with Bayley Park was maintained by his daughter Anne who in 1776 became the second wife of John Trayton Fuller. He was a cousin of the renowned John Fuller of Brightling known to posterity as 'Jolly Jack' or 'Mad Jack' Fuller whose architectural follies remain a feature of the local countryside. Eliott paid a dowry of £3000, and promised a further similar sum on his death, in the meantime making a substantial loan of £15,000 to his son-in-law. The newly-married couple moved into Bayley Park where they had seven children in quick succession - Augustus Eliot (June 1777), Elizabeth Ann (July 1780), Francis John (March 1782), Sarah Maria (April 1783), Thomas Trayton (February 1785), William Stephen (March 1788) and Rose Henry (March 1789).[16]

Eliott's only son, Francis Augustus, followed in his father's footsteps into the army, and was serving as an aide-de-camp to George III when his father died. But having inherited the title, the second Lord Heathfield decided against keeping Bayley Park. This was because he was also in line to inherit the more important Drake estates in Devonshire from his maternal uncle, Sir Francis Henry Drake, the fifth and last baronet. This he duly did four years later in 1794, and it was there that he established his country base. He continued to pursue his military career with success, becoming a general in 1808 and Colonel of the 1st Dragoon Guards before his death in 1813. Today he is probably better remembered through the equestrian portraits which he commissioned from the Swiss-born artist Jacques-Laurant Agasse. However, when they were exhibited in 1989 at the Tate Gallery one critic observed that 'the horse is depicted with meticulous accuracy if not relish, in contrast to the rider, who seems to be included only to show off the mount'.[17]

The executors of his father's will put Bayley Park on the market at an auction advertised for midday on Friday 2 September 1791 at Garraway's Coffee House, Exchange Alley, in Cornhill. The Eliott connection with Heathfield was about to end.[18]

The 17th c. mansion
Painting attributed to Gerard van Edema

The new approach to the house proposed by Humphry Repton
(From his Red Book, 1794)

View of the Park
(From Repton's Red Book)

View towards the Gibraltar Tower
(From Repton's Red Book)

View of Trees in the Park by William Crotch (1809)

Vale of Heathfield by J.M.W. Turner (c. 1815)

A reception room today

Andreas and Inger Ugland and family

7. THE PARK IN ITS HEYDAY: FRANCIS NEWBERY (1791–1818)

The sale of the Park in 1791 took place just two years after the outbreak of the French revolution: the new owner's tenure was to coincide very closely with the revolutionary period and the renewed and prolonged conflict with France which arose out of it. These events provided not only the background to this phase in the story of the Park: they also had some direct and tangible effects on it and Lord Heathfield's successor, Francis Newbery.

Initial reactions to events in France had been predominantly favourable and even ecstatic: in Wordsworth's famous couplet 'Bliss was it in that dawn to be alive, But to be young was very heaven !' The French, it seemed, had at last seen the light: the summoning of the Estates General, the storming of the Bastille, and the promulgation of the Rights of Man were seen as a triumph for those freedoms which Britons had long enjoyed and – as in the case of Tom Paine (a one-time Lewes resident) – evidence of the superiority of democratic forms of government.

But Edmund Burke, in his *Reflections on the Revolution in France* published in 1790 had already warned about the consequences of upturning an established order, and of the danger of anarchy and a new despotism. Soon events appeared to confirm his worst fears. In 1793 Louis XVI and his wife Marie Antoinette were sent to the guillotine; a Reign of Terror was imposed on the country, which eventually destroyed even its own promoters; and the restoration of order later in the decade brought to power Napoleon Buonaparte who then proceeded in a series of brilliant military campaigns to impose his will over most of Europe.

IMPACT OF THE FRENCH REVOLUTION

These developments had several important repercussions in Sussex. In the first place, those in power and positions of authority in the county, as elsewhere, became very nervous as they saw the old order being swept away first in France itself and then throughout much of the continent. They feared the same thing might happen in Britain. As we shall see, the new owner of the Park shared these concerns and took steps to align himself publicly with the defenders of law and order.

There was a second, and even more direct effect on the county. In 1793 the Jacobin government in Paris declared war on Britain, opening a long period of hostilities which was to last, with only a brief interruption, for twenty-two years. As on many other occasions in the past, Sussex then became part of the country's front-line. During this period there was a serious threat of invasion on two different occasions. This meant a heavy concentration of troops in the coastal areas; the large-scale mobilisation of volunteers and the gentry to lead them; and the construction of new defences, including the still-familiar Martello towers. It also meant for a great deal of the time much danger for coastal and Channel shipping and, as the Napoleonic blockade was imposed, more incentive and opportunities for the county's smugglers.

The conflict with France also had other economic and social effects on the county. This time it did not profit from the much increased demand for arma-ments: by now the Wealden iron industry was in terminal decline as a result of competition from the new technology being used in the Midlands, Wales, and the North. The last furnace at Ashburnham closed down in 1813. But the Weald nevertheless profited in other ways from wartime needs. The threat of food shortages gave a further boost to the expansion of agriculture in the county which had begun towards the middle of the 18th century under the impact of a growing population. This was particularly felt in the Weald where more land was brought into production through enclosure of common land and pasture was converted into arable land.

Some of the most intensive new developments took place along the ridges between Cross in Hand and Burwash and between Heathfield and Battle, lead-ing to new settlements at Burwash Weald and Woods Corner. At the same time yields of grains, root-crops and hops increased through new techniques as practised by the Fullers at Heathfield and elsewhere.[1]

The Weald nevertheless remained an area where landholdings were much smaller and ownership much more fragmented than elsewhere in the county. At the beginning of the 18th century, for instance, there were more than a hundred different owners in the Heathfield area, and between 1796 and 1806 the number of separate units of taxable land increased from 161 to 199.[2]

The rapid development of a network of turnpike roads in the second half of the 18th century was now helping to open up the Weald which for so long had remained backward and undeveloped. Travelling times from London had been reduced from a day - or longer in bad weather - to a few hours. So although it remained a haunt for highwaymen and robbers, a contemporary advertisement claimed that Sussex now possessed 'every requisite for either res-idence or investment'.[3]

THE PARK IN 1791

The particulars of the sale of 'Baily Park' described it as 'a valuable and most desirable' estate consisting of 'a Capital Mansion House' with 'numerous offices, beautiful and extensive pleasure-grounds, lawn, plantations, park and woodlands, and sundry adjoining farms'. In all, the estate covered thirteen hundred and seventy eight acres, with an annual rental value of five hundred and seventy pounds. The sale details went on to describe the 'Capital and Modern Mansion' as being 'in complete Repair and fit for the immediate Reception of a Family'. The ground floor offered a set of good-sized but not huge rooms - 'an Eating-room' (32 x 24ft), a drawing room (24 x 22ft), a library or breakfast room (22 x 16ft), a dressing room, a commodious Hall, a handsome principal stair-case and 'a back ditto'. On the first floor were five good bedrooms, a dressing room and closets with attics above for the servants, while in the basement there was the kitchen, housekeeper's rooms, servants hall, other domestic offices and dry cellaring.

Outside there was 'excellent stabling for sixteen horses', a double coach-house for six carriages, 'a very large and capital Riding-house, lately built at great Expense', a farmhouse including a dairy, brew-house and laundry, a walled farmyard, a barn, granary and 'other Useful and Convenient Buildings', together with a two-acre kitchen garden, mostly walled and 'planted with the choicest Fruit-trees in great Perfection'.

Next came the 'Pleasure Grounds and Lawn' described as 'beautiful and extensive, and remarkably well disposed with numerous shady Walks and Shrubberies, and ornamented with Plantations of lofty Timber; Fish ponds well stocked, and supplied by a fine Rivulet that runs through the Centre of the Park; contiguous to which are some fine Plantations and Woodlands and a small convenient Farm'.

In addition, there was a considerable estate let out to tenants: this consisted of several farms, a number of cottages with gardens, the Half Moon Inn, and various pieces of land.[4]

Apart from the intrinsic merits of the mansion, the agreeable nature of its immediate surroundings and the substantial estate which Eliott had built up, there can be little doubt that its association with a noble patriot greatly added to its allure. And to none more so than Francis Newbery, another in the line of successful City men who had been attracted by Bayley Park. It is just possible that he may have been aware of it from another source: there was a connection between the Heathfield area and the booksellers and publishers of St Paul's Churchyard (where he was then living) going back to the end of the

PARTICULARS,

AND

CONDITIONS of SALE,

OF A VALUABLE AND MOST DESIRABLE

FREEHOLD and COPYHOLD ESTATE,

CALLED

B A I L Y   P A R K,

SITUATE IN THE

PARISH of *HEATHFIELD*, in the COUNTY of *SUSSEX*,

15 Miles from *East Bourn* and *Hastings*, 15 from *Lewes*, and 51 from *London*;

CONSISTING OF

A CAPITAL MANSION HOUSE,

(The Refidence of the late RIGHT HONOURABLE *LORD HEATHFIELD*, deceafed)

WITH NUMEROUS OFFICES,

BEAUTIFUL AND EXTENSIVE PLEASURE-GROUNDS, LAWN,
PLANTATIONS, PARK, AND WOODLANDS,

AND SUNDRY ADJOINING FARMS,

CONTAINING

THIRTEEN HUNDRED AND SEVENTY-SEVEN ACRES;

Of which   Acres are COPYHOLD;

The annual Value of the whole (exclufive of the Manfion) being

FIVE HUNDRED AND SEVENTY POUNDS:

Which will be SOLD by AUCTION,

By Mr. *Y O U N G*,

At *Garraway*'s Coffee-Houfe, *Exchange Alley, Cornhill*, LONDON,

On FRIDAY the 2d Day of *SEPTEMBER*, 1791, at Twelve o'Clock,

IN ONE LOT,

BY ORDER OF THE EXECUTORS OF

The late RIGHT HONOURABLE *LORD HEATHFIELD*, deceafed.

Printed PARTICULARS may be had at the Star, *Lewes*; Swan, *Haftings*; Caftle, *Brightbelmftone*; Crown, *Tunbridge Wells*; *King's Head Canterbury*; Star, *Maidftone*; at *Garraway's*; of Mr. RICHARDSON, Surveyor, Manor Houfe, *Chelfea*; and of Mr. YOUNG, No 58, *Chancery-Lane, London*, where a Plan of the Eftate may be feen.

Mr. JOHN UPWRIGHT, of *Heathfield*, will fhew the Manfion and Eftate.

17th century when Richard Wilkin, the son of a long-serving vicar of Heathfield, became a distinguished member of that London society, while maintaining a house at Warbleton.

At all events, Newbery visited Bayley Park with his wife and children on 3 August 1791 to view it, had dinner with the vicar of Heathfield the Rev. Richard Constable, and then made a successful bid for the estate. On 12 August he signed a contract to buy it for £17,500. Some six weeks later, on 29 September, the new owner took possession.[5]

FRANCIS NEWBERY

Francis Newbery was a man of many parts: a scholar, a poet, an amateur musician of considerable accomplishment, a devotee of amateur theatricals, and an ardent sportsman. He was also a man of considerable wealth and ambition, the former being derived in large part from the sale of patent medicines, then as now a lucrative trade. He was forty-eight when he became the owner of Bayley Park, having been born in Reading on 6 July 1743, the youngest of three children.

His father, John Newbery, came from a line of booksellers and had married the widow of a printer and newspaper editor. He had begun the hard way, travelling around the country to sell his books, and although he was to pursue this activity with vigour and increasing success, in the year when Francis was born, perhaps feeling the need for extra income, he also expanded into the patent medicine business. He then paid £100 for a fourteen-year licence to sell certain 'female pills'. A year later he opened a warehouse in the City, and in 1745 moved from Reading into St Paul's Churchyard in the City.[6]

As Francis grew up, his father prospered. He was a talented entrepreneur with a flair for developing new markets. In addition to selling books, he launched out into a number of publishing ventures. First came childrens' books; then, in partnership with a relative, a popular threepenny periodical called 'The Midwife, or The Old Woman's Magazine' full of coarse humour (which they wrote themselves). Later, in 1758, he branched out again with the first of several weekly newspapers and broadsheets. But at the same time his publishing business allowed him to cultivate serious men of letters. He become, for instance, a friend of Dr Johnson who in turn introduced him to Oliver Goldsmith, whose novel *The Vicar of Wakefield* he published in 1766. He also acquired a reputation as a 'philanthropic publisher', lending money to both men, and employing Tobias Smollett, the author of *Clarissa* and other novels, when he was in prison.

Francis Newbery

At the same time his patent medicine business was flourishing. When John Newbery arrived in London he was already selling over thirty different pills and potions. He became a friend of Dr Robert James who like Dr Johnson came from Lichfield in Staffordshire, and began to market the fever powder for which James took out a patent in November 1746. This soon became a very popular nostrum for a wide range of disorders including fever, gout, rheumatism, other inflammatory diseases, measles, pleurisy, and sore throats. To this best-seller other and more exotic remedies were then added. In 1757, for example, he concluded an agreement for the manufacture and marketing of the Lisbon or German Doctor's Diet-Drink, the Angola Ptisan, and the Unguents de Cao – the latter reputedly being made by first drowning a 'good fat young dog' in two gallons of water, adding other unlikely ingredients, and then boiling and straining.[7]

The popularity of such doubtful remedies has to be seen against the background of the relatively primitive state of medical knowledge at the time and the prevalence of many fatal or disabling diseases which frequently reached epidemic proportions. The young Francis Newbery himself suffered from a severe attack of smallpox at an early age and almost lost the use of his left eye. It was in the hope of curing its ill effects that he was first sent to school at the age of eight or nine to Ramsgate on the Kent coast. Sea-bathing was then just becoming popular as a remedy for many ailments, promoted by the Lewes doctor, Richard Russell. (It was his move in the mid 1750s to Brighthelmstone which led to its rapid development into the resort of Brighton, much favoured by the Prince Regent). But the young Newbery stayed only two years at Ramsgate grammar school: he then went on to a private school at Hoddesdon in Hertfordshire, and from there in 1758 into the fifth form at Merchant Taylors in the City.

He was clearly a young man of spirit as well as wide interests: in his autobiography he recalls having enjoyed mimicking the headmaster, Mr Criche. And when in 1762, at the age of nineteen, he became an undergraduate at Trinity College, Oxford intending to read for a degree in medicine he spent a great deal of time on other pursuits – music, poetry, amateur dramatics, and membership of a student club called the Jelly Bag society. He was told off by the great Dr Johnson for spending so much time playing the violin: 'Young man', he said, 'give the fiddle to the first beggar man you meet, or you will never be a scholar'.[8]

Newbery spent four years at Oxford, during which time he certainly devoted some attention to medicine: he records, for instance, that during the winter months of his third and fourth years he became a pupil at Dr Hunter's celebrated Anatomical School in London. But in 1766 he quit Oxford and went to Cambridge, becoming a Fellow Commoner at Sidney Sussex College, apparently because he could get a degree in physic there three years earlier than in the other place. But he continued to play the violin, to write poetry, and to take an interest in many other things. He became friendly, for instance, with Dr Richard Farmer, Master of Emmanuel and the Librarian of the university, and with him and his former Oxford tutor visited the principal libraries of the colleges.

Mary Newbery

The following year his father died, leaving him part of the bookselling and the whole of the patent medicine business. After taking Dr Johnson's advice, Francis Newbery abandoned Cambridge and his medical studies to return to London. For the next thirteen years he continued both as a publisher and as a supplier of patent medicines: he did particularly well by acquiring the rights to a new medicine, the 'Analeptic Pill' which was used as a general tonic. But he also ran into a spot of bother: Dr James's fever powder which he supplied to Oliver Goldsmith was held by some to be responsible for the latter's death in 1774. Newbery defended himself vigorously both in the press and in a voluminous treatise about the product which he published.[9]

The incident does not seem to have done him any lasting harm. Five years later, in 1779, he moved into a substantial new house he had built on the north-east side of St Paul's which also served as his business premises and warehouse for Dr James's Powder. It was at this time that he decided to relinquish publishing and concentrate on selling medicines, a decision praised by Dr Johnson at the house-warming. According to Newbery's account, the good doctor 'expressed much satisfaction on finding that the trade had

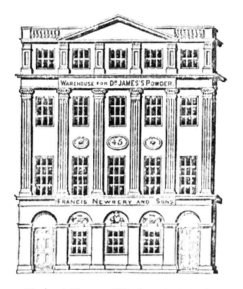

WAREHOUSE FOR Dr JAMES'S POWDER.

FRANCIS NEWBERY AND SONS

Newbery's House and Warehouse in St Paul's Churchyard

produced so good an establishment' and when he was thanked for the advice which had led to the decision Johnson observed: 'Sir, it could not be wrong; the only difficulty was that of detaching your mind from literary occupations and in relinquishing a profession for a shop. You had the good sense to surmount it, and now after having had the education, you are enabled, by your father's industry and your own, to lead the life of a gentleman'.[10]

It was no doubt in pursuit of that style of life that twelve years later Francis Newbery bought Bayley Park. He had developed a taste for hunting, which up to that point he had satisfied by keeping horses at Croydon. In the meantime he had become well established in the City where he had been admitted to the livery of the Goldsmiths' Company in 1781. He had also by then an extensive family. He was married at Bath in May 1770 to Mary Raikes, the sister of the founder of Sunday schools: they had four sons and two daughters. Their eldest daughter, Mary, was already twenty when they moved to Heathfield and two of their sons - John and Robert - were in their teens. But the other members of the family were considerably younger: Charlotte was eleven, William only four, and Charles even younger.

NEWBERY MAKES HIS MARK

Once the purchase had been completed Newbery began, as Lucas put it, 'to seek outlets for his wealth and enterprise'. As the house was in such good order his attention focussed initially on the park, where he set out both to perpetuate the fame of the first Lord Heathfield and at the same time to make the Park worthy of its new owner.

One of the first things he did was to change its name from Bayley to Heathfield Park. In this way he neatly combined a clearer territorial identification for it with a name that also reminded everyone of his illustrious predecessor. The change seems to have been accepted quite readily: the park already figures under its new name on a map of the area published just three years later in 1795 by Gardner and Green.

In the meantime Newbery had taken another important initiative. He must have laid his plans well in advance, for building work began on a tower to commemorate the defence of Gibraltar on 2 March 1792 following his purchase the previous autumn. The chosen site lay on an area of prominent heathland, some 600 feet above sea level, just beyond the north-western boundary of the Park and on land held as copyhold of the Manor of Laughton. Lord Pelham, the lord of the manor, gave the freehold as his contribution. The tower, 55 feet high, was built of stone, quarried it is said by Jonathan Harmer of the famous local family: it took just over eighteen months to complete and cost £3000. It was built to dominate the local landscape, and to last: though it is currently in urgent need of attention, it is still there.

The Gibraltar Tower has an octagonal base and a circular main section capped by a battlement, from which there are very extensive views which on a good day can extend to 30-35 miles over Kent, Sussex, and Surrey and the Channel - taking in (it is claimed) as many as forty churches. Over the door giving access to the Tower there was placed a tablet with the inscription

The Gibraltar Tower

'Calpes Defensori' ('To the Defender of Gibraltar'), the letters of which were formed from metal of guns from the Spanish floating batteries. Inside a circular staircase gave access to three rooms which were later furnished with memorabilia of General Eliott and the siege. The completion of the building on 26 October 1793 was celebrated by an article in the *Gentleman's Magazine*, and no doubt also by Newbery himself.[11]

HUMPHRY REPTON AND THE PARK

At an early stage Newbery re-introduced deer to the Park, and erected a pale fence around it to keep them in. But this was only a first step in his plans for it. He then called in the most fashionable landscape architect of the day, Humphry Repton, to advise him on what other improvements should be made.

This was a period when the emphasis in England had shifted from the construction of formal gardens based on continental models to the creation of

picturesque landscapes. But in the case of Bayley (now Heathfield) Park the
formal gardens do not seem, from the evidence we currently have, ever to have
been a major feature, and the configuration and layout of the park at the time
Newbery inherited it were already very much in line with the new thinking.
This was almost certainly by accident rather than design. As we have seen, the
park had already been in existence for almost two hundred years, and possibly
for very much longer. It probably acquired its appearance by an essentially
natural process over the years supplemented by the occasional intervention of
its successive owners. There is no evidence, at all events, that any single person
had been responsible for the design of the park in the past. But, as Repton
rapidly discovered, nature had done its job so well that there was not a great
deal that even he could suggest to improve it.

Repton inspected Heathfield Park early in April 1794, and submitted his
report on 29 April in one of his famous 'Red Books' which set out his reason-
ing and recommendations, accompanied by a series of watercolour sketches,
some with tuck-in flaps showing 'before' and 'after' *(See colour section)*.

As a practised hand in dealing with owners, he was suitably deferential –
and even obsequious– in presenting his conclusions which were designed to
flatter as well as persuade. From the beginning, however, the message was
plain. In the first part of his report he wrote in glowing terms about the natural
beauty of the Park in a famous passage which is frequently quoted as typical
of Repton's philosophy and approach:[12]

> 'Heathfield Park is one of those subjects from whence my art
> can derive little credit: because the world is apt to delight in
> 'alteration' rather than improvement, and to applaud every
> change, altho' no higher beauty is produced by it, than Nature
> herself presents to the prying and inquisitive eye of her enthusi-
> astic votaries.
>
> The Character and Situation of this park are strictly in har-
> mony with each other; both are magnificent and splendid, yet a
> degree of elegance and beauty prevails which is rarely to be
> found where greatness of character and loftiness of situation are
> the most obvious features because magnificence is not always
> compatible with convenience, nor vast extent of prospect with
> interesting scenes of beauty.
>
> The power of Art can do but little towards improving by
> *alteration* the natural advantages of Heathfield park; and it is rather
> the duty of the improver to avail himself of those charms which
> Nature has profusely scattered; he must lead the stranger to the

most pleasing stations, and call his attention to those objects
which from their novelty, variety, contrasts or combination, are
most likely to interest and delight the mind.

On this foundation ought to be built the future improvement
of Heathfield park; not by doing violence to its Native Genius, but
after sedulously studying the beauties of the place, and connect
them with other in lines the most easy, natural and graceful'.

Repton then went on, nevertheless, to make a considerable number of
recommendations. The first proposed the construction of a new approach to
the Park and its house. 'I have frequently observed', he wrote, 'that a good
approach actually stamped the whole character of a place'. But he disagreed
both with those who thought that an approach should not display 'much or
even any' of the scenery and also those who 'with equal absurdity conduct the
stranger by a violently circuitous route to show all its beauties, leaving nothing
to be seen after we have reached the door of the mansion'.

In his view it was important first to consider 'the natural character and situation of the place'. If, as was the case with Heathfield Park, its beauties were
'many and conspicuous', and could already be glimpsed from the road, 'it would
be an unpardonable economy to refuse the visitor a way through the park to the

The new approach to the house (from Repton's Red Book)

house'. Yet this was precisely what the existing approach did, following the road round the northern boundary of the Park where it was largely hidden from view by 'a long skreen of plantation', then entering it from the east (as does the present main entrance, opposite the Community College), where the house was closest to its boundary. 'Thus we purposely go round the place, to discover its defects, lest we should form too favourable an opinion of its advantages'.

To improve the approach he first suggested that a triangular plantation should be introduced to divide the high road from the one leading to the park. It would also become a feature of the place, and help to unite the Tower which 'at present scarse appears to belong to the Park' with the rest of it. But 'in scenery which is naturally grand' the new entrance (where the North Lodge is now located) should be neither too obtrusive nor 'the affected humility of a thatched cottage': he proposed therefore a 'neat simple building of sufficient size to hold the Gatekeeper and his little family'.

View from library
(from Repton's Red Book)

Beyond the lodge he suggested that a new plantation should be established to take the new approach road further into the park before sweeping eastwards along the brow of the hill towards the house. It would then descend gently into the intervening glen towards a group of large beeches, guarded by a post and rail fence ('the appearance of such a precaution adds greatly to the romantic idea of its necessity'). The stone quarry under an oak to the left of the road 'will engage the attention for a while, till the vast scene at once bursts upon the sight'. The way out of the valley would be 'so conducted' that the house would be concealed by a small group of trees 'till at length it presents itself under their branches'. Following round the head of the valley the road would bring the visitor 'up to the portico at a proper angle to show it well in perspective'.

Repton then turned to consider the views from the house. His most radical proposal was to remove a line of tall firs which largely obscured the view southwards from the house across the park towards the sea. 'They are enormous trees, but have outgrown their beauty and depress the consequence of every other object near them: the house and even vast oaks and beeches in their neighbourhood suffer by comparison'. He also proposed getting rid of the nearby pond which he found 'defective, because it obstructs the eye in viewing what is beyond it', and removing a brick wall so that the lawn could be extended. He illustrated the impact of the suggested changes by a watercolour sketch, and with another showed the view from the library, through the colonnade in the foreground, which he had found 'so peculiarly striking by moonlight'.

He also made a series of proposals to improve the view from the drawing room. The existing outlook, he said, was 'defective in composition' as it involved too many parallel lines all of which 'appear to fall in a sloping direction'. He suggested that it needed a counterpoise, which was to be achieved by drawing attention to the Tower. In the foreground there should be a small group of trees and beyond them some single specimens, while in the middle distance the wood on the far side of the glen should be cleared to open up a view of the Tower which in turn would be highlighted against the trees of a new plantation to be established close by. This, he

The mansion in 1794
(from Repton's Red Book)

wrote 'will contribute to balance the landscape, while it connects the Tower with the park and leads the eye to the summit of the hill by a continuity of wood'.

His concern to find ways of better integrating the Gibraltar Tower with the rest of the park also led him to suggest a new and more direct path from the house. Walks, he wrote 'may be discussed under two distinct heads: those for use and those for beauty: the first are for the family, and the others for strangers'. The tower, he went, on 'is rather at too great a distance to be a common walk' but a shorter approach could be made by a branch from the new approach road crossing the intervening valley 'by quick windings or where the banks are steep, a few steps might be introduced'.

Repton also proposed making several short additions to other existing drives to open up new views and vistas, several of which he illustrated with his watercolour drawings. But he confessed that his painterly skills could not hope to do justice to the prospect from the Gibraltar Tower. He nevertheless painted a view of the house seen through one of the roundel windows which must have given his patron much satisfaction, as his final words about the tower were certainly also calculated to do:

> 'I must not dismiss this subject without expressing the pleasure which was excited in me, on finding a lofty Tower consecrated as a tribute of gratitude for his public services, to that Gallant Commander who derived his title from Heathfield and his military glory from the Rock of Gibraltar'.

There were also several reminders in the book about the distinguished company Newbery could now count himself to be among as a patron of Repton's skills. When, for instance, he discussed the provision of seats along the walks, he quoted at some length from the Red Book which the Prime Minister of the day, William Pitt, had commissioned him to prepare for his country seat at Holwood, Kent. There Repton had set out his theory about the role of seats in a country park. They had, he argued, four purposes: rest, enjoyment of a view, ornament, and 'a charm to beguile the weary and insensibly to seduce the indolent stranger to the next bench'. He made a number of proposals about where they should be sited in Heathfield Park, including one in a rotunda to provide shelter from the elements.

He turned, finally, to the 'more sequestered and not less pleasing scenes within the deep recesses of the wooded glen', and in particular to the line of small lakes which had been created to provide water-power for Heathfield furnace. Repton was not concerned with their utility but their decorative function. He observed that 'a broad sheet of water is a delightful circumstance', but nevertheless decided against trying to link up three of the ponds: it would be, he wrote, 'so violent an operation that it ought not to be attempted'. The most he thought should be done was to create 'an apparent union' of two of them on different levels with the help of a dam which would be disguised as a bridge. He also suggested, but rather tentatively, that the water from the spring feeding the lakes might be 'conducted through small channels from a high level and made to fall in tinkling rills or foaming cascades, over ledges of rocks to be prepared for its reception...This delightful management of *living water* is infinitely preferable to the dull sleepy surface of a *stagnant pool,*and may be varied in so many different manners, as to yield endless sources of pleasure'.

Newbery was no doubt suitable flattered by Repton's conclusions: the highest accolade had been bestowed on Heathfield Park by the most fashionable of experts. That was probably more important to him than any of the specific recommendations - and it is not clear how many of these he actually carried out. He certainly did construct the suggested new approach to the house, and commissioned John Crunden, a prominent architect who had been born in Sussex, to design the North Lodge at its entrance. There is evidence, too, of a 13-acre plantation by the tower, and a bridge across the point joining two of the lakes. He probably also carried out some of the minor alterations to improve the view towards the south from the house.

Even today, after many further changes of ownership and sundry other vicissitudes, like the great storm of 1987, the general configuration of the park is still recognisably the same as at this period. And although it owed much more to Nature and the passage of time than to Repton himself, the fact that he approved of it in such eloquent terms has served to preserve it in the intervening period and has also provided, in recent years, a powerful argument against a number of proposed developments which would certainly have laid waste to a substantial part of it.[13]

THE JACK CADE MONUMENT

As part of his quest for greater renown both for himself and for Heathfield, Newbery - looking beyond the confines of the park itself - decided to erect another monument. This was to commemorate the reputed capture of Jack Cade at Heathfield in 1450. He probably had two aims in mind. One was to give a further historical dimension to his chosen country seat which otherwise, until its association with General Eliott, had little to be remembered for. But at least as important was the message that Newbery wished to send to his peers and neighbours that he was on the side of law and order at a time of revolution. This was clearly spelled out on the wording of the stone tablet attached to the side of the simple, rather sombre stone pedestal:

> 'Near this spot was slain the notorious rebel Jack Cade by Alexander Iden, Sheriff of Kent, AD1450. His body was carried to London, and his head fixed upon London Bridge. This is the success of all rebels, and this fortune chanceth ever to traitors - *Hall's Chronicle*'.

This monument was erected on the site where Cade was supposed to have been captured, raised up on a bank on the north side of the ridge road from Heathfield to Battle close to the site where the fairs and markets were held. Up to then this had been known as Catte Street: here too Newbery was anxious to leave his footprint in the history of the locality even if it meant, perversely, also perpetuating its connection with a rebel. Henceforth that part of the ridgeway was to be known – as it still is – as Cade Street.

THE ESTATE ENLARGED

Newbery also very considerably extended the estate during his twenty-eight years of ownership. He added to the 1378 acres he had bought from Lord Heathfield to make a total of just over two thousand. He also substantially increased the acreage under direct management - from 550 to 927 - which included not only newly enclosed land around the Gibraltar Tower, but also large tracts of woodland and plantations which formed part of a number of farms whose land was otherwise rented out. These included Binglett, Broomham, Cold Hill, Gameland, Greenwood, Holeban, Hugglett, Kiln, and Little Tottingforth. He also purchased and managed Marklye wood

A woodland view in the Park (From Repton's Red Book)

ESRO AMS 6310

88

(almost 140 acres) and 120 acres of woodland of Newick farm. The rest of that farm (some 166 acres) he rented out, together with other farms he bought, including Broomham, Milkhurst, Street End and Mill. In all, by the end of his period at the park, he was renting out 1156 acres at an annual rental of just over £920.[14]

An estate of this size generated a good deal of administrative and legal work, and Newbery's solicitors were kept busy. In 1797, for instance, 'Jolly Jack' Fuller threatened litigation over the supply of water to his land from the ponds in the park, a claim going back to the agreement with Raymond Blackmore in 1721, even though the furnace had long ceased its activity. There was also a flurry of activity when brown coal (lignite) was found in the Park and elsewhere in the district. Various mineral and mining experts were called in, and gave favourable opinions, and on this occasion Fuller and Newbery were at one in seeking to exploit this new resource. But it appears that threats of legal action by those in the coal trade were made, and ridicule poured on the scheme, Jonathan Harmer himself being called 'a pudding head' and being asked 'How long have you been a coal merchant ?' At all events, the matter was not pursued.[15]

There was a more positive outcome, however, of another venture in which Newbery and Fuller were involved, this time in company with the Earl of Ashburnham and Sir Godfrey Webster of Battle. This was the promotion and construction of the turnpike road between Heathfield and Beach Down at Battle (with a spur also to Robertsbridge) for which the necessary parliamentary Act was passed in 1813. This was a rather late addition to the network of such roads which had begun to serve the Heathfield area since the mid 1750s – but nevertheless a further welcome addition to the improvement of communications in the district which for so many centuries had been so bad.

PUBLIC LIFE: A MUTINY AND AFTER

Newbery's commitment to his country seat seems to have cut short what could have been, had he so chosen, a promising career in the public life of the City. He had become a liveryman of the Goldsmiths' Company in 1781 and in 1793 he was elected to its Court of Assistants. Two years later he was approached to consider standing in a by-election as a candidate for Parliament for the City. According to his own account, he would have been able to count on support from Dissenters as well as friends at the Bank and the Stock Exchange in spite of being asked to stand as a Tory. However, after reflection, he decided not to do so, and 'Heathfield certainly had its weight in the decision'.[16]

He soon found, however, that his services were in demand there, too. Like his predecessor at the Park, John Trayton Fuller, he was asked to become a Justice of the Peace, as there was none other within many miles and, as he explained, 'the roads were at particular seasons almost impracticable'. At the beginning of 1795 he was appointed Sheriff for the county. This came at a time when there was widespread public unrest due to the soaring price of bread. Newbery was at once faced by a potentially serious threat to public order. On April 17, while he was at Quarter Sessions in Lewes to take his oath of office, news came of a mutiny of the Oxfordshire Militia stationed at Blatchington barracks on the coast. These troops were part of the forces that had been assembled to deal with the threat from revolutionary France. But complaining of the high price of bread and inadequate pay they had marched off in a body to seize corn and flour in the tide mill at Bishopstone and on a ship at Newhaven.

The Lancashire Fencible Cavalry was despatched to deal with them, and eventually the militia were persuaded to return to their barracks. But the situation was still very tense when Newbery, accompanying Lord Sheffield, went late that evening to Newhaven. Their chaise was surrounded by soldiers with fixed bayonets when it arrived at the inn. Having given orders for the navy to guard the ordnance ship in port they then returned to Lewes - only to learn that the mutineers intended to march on the town the following day.

The cavalry was ordered back to Newhaven at break of day, accompanied by a party of horse artillery. Soon the rebellious Oxfordshire troops were observed advancing in a column over the hill, and deploying into line when they became aware of their opponents. The situation was sufficiently threatening for the artillery to be ordered to fire two or three shots over their heads. The mutineers then broke ranks and retreated. They were rounded up by the cavalry and forced to surrender their arms. Clearly troubled by this experience, Newbery wrote: 'Thus ended an insurrection, more formidable in its aspect than any we have witnessed of late years, excepting the mutiny in our fleet. The monster was extinguished in its birth'.[17]

Although twopence a day 'bread money' was added to the soldiers' pay, severe retribution also followed. A court martial condemned two of the ringleaders to death, and six to be flogged. At a special Assize in Lewes at the end of the following month two more received death sentences. Afterwards Newbery entertained the judges and some of their attendants for two days at Heathfield Park on their way back to London. But that was not the end of the affair. Once back in town he learned from the Under-Sheriff that there was 'some murmuring and disaffection' at Horsham - where two of the executions were to take place – against both the sentences and the high price of bread. He feared that there might be disturbances and an attempt to rescue the condemned men. Newbery decided to be present himself, and to call out the yeomanry commanded by Trayton Fuller and another local squire.

On the appointed day, Saturday 13 June, Newbery also had to witness the carrying out of the sentences decreed by the court martial. This took place at Goldstone Bottom, close to Brighton. About six thousand troops were present. 'The scene', he wrote, 'was truly grand, awful and impressive'. Three of the men condemned to flogging each received some 200 lashes, 'which seemed from their cries to be very severe'. About a dozen of those who had been foremost were then hauled forward to form the firing squad to carry out the two death sentences. Only one of the men was killed instantly; the other 'in great agony turned upon his back'. His misery was only ended when another shot was fired close into his ears. The assembled troops were then marched round the dead bodies as they lay on the ground.

Immediately afterwards, Newbery had to return to Brighton and take a chaise on to Horsham to witness the execution of the other two soldiers. There the two troops of yeomanry cavalry which had been mobilised for the occasion proved sufficient to quell any attempt at trouble. 'Not a symptom of dissatisfaction appeared among the multitude', wrote Newbery, 'and the unfortunate men, after being conducted with solemn ceremony to the fatal spot, and a short time spent in prayer, submitted to their fate with calmness and resignation, acknowledging the justice of their sentence. Thus ended this very alarming and dangerous insurrection'.[18]

It is clear from Newbery's comments that this first practical experience as a defender of law and order at a particularly turbulent time made a deep impression on him. He appears to have been genuinely shocked by the brutality involved in repression. His continuing work as a JP also led him to a concern with the welfare of the poorer members of society, as he explained in a pamphlet on the income tax he published in 1801 in which he also set out a *Short Scheme for meliorating the Condition of the Labouring Man*. The idea he put forward, to supplement the poor rate by direct relief at times of high bread prices, had arisen he said 'from what I have had the opportunity of observing by acting as a magistrate in the county in which I reside, where the lower order of people are numerous; where no manufactures are carried on; where labourers are scantily paid; and where the poor-rates, even in ordinary times, amount to half the rack-rents'.[19]

Newbery was also a Commissioner of Taxes, and put forward ideas to ease the tax burden on tradespeople, arguing that the system was skewed in favour of landowners' interests. But, after his torrid year as Sheriff, he does not appear to have advanced further into the higher realms of public life in the county. He did not stand for parliament, and he does not appear to have played any prominent part in the political life of the county. Nor did he receive any honours, as he may well have hoped for in his early years, when he made his mark with such éclat at Heathfield Park. It may simply be that, as a newcomer to Sussex and as a man of recently-acquired wealth (and that largely based on the sale of patent medicines), he was not sufficiently acceptable to the established landowners who were firmly entrenched in positions of power and influence. As always, Heathfield was a rather peripheral place as far as the affairs of the county, and its county town, were concerned. It may also be that his tender conscience and reforming tendencies did not recommend him for further preferment at a time of continuing social tension.

At all events, the remaining twenty three-years of his life appear to have been devoted, apart from his work as a magistrate, essentially to his family, his business affairs, and his estate.[20]

PRIVATE PURSUITS AT THE PARK

Newbery was certainly a devoted family man: he used to turn the Riding School into a theatre where his children performed plays. 'The idea of getting up a little comic piece during the Christmas holidays', he wrote, 'originated with the young people, for the amusement of themselves and the neighbours, many of whom had never seen a theatrical performance, and when the Author found how well the parts were conceived and executed, he gave every aid and encouragement to the design by erecting a small stage in a large room, and by writing the Prologue and Epilogue'. The verses he wrote to introduce *The Midnight Hour* which was performed on 3 January 1793 have survived. Spoken by his fourth son Charles, they began:[21]

> 'So you're all met! *(coming forward)* and each has got his seat:
> With rare keen appetite for this new treat.
> I'm glad to see you. What a crowd I view !
> So, Tom! Ah, cousin Martha! How do you do ?'

There was much more in similar vein in what the author himself described as 'rude verse and doggerel rhime'. But it clearly went down well, and the following Christmas Newbery wrote the epilogue for a production of Macklin's *Love à la Mode*. These pieces were printed by the author for private circulation in 1815 together with some of his other verses, which included 'A Farewell to Heathfield Park' and 'The Return to Heathfield Park'. These last two were set to music as glees by Dr William Crotch, a musician of great distinction. He had been an infant prodigy who at the age of four was already performing in London on the organ and piano. Subsequently, at the age of 22 he became professor of music at Oxford, and later, in 1822, he was to become the first Principal of the Royal Academy of Music.

William Crotch was also an accomplished amateur painter, and a friend of John Constable. Although some thirty years younger than Newbery, he and his family seem to have become good friends with the owner of Heathfield Park, for we know that they stayed there in August 1809 and again in the same month two years later. On both occasions he produced a number of very attractive watercolours of the park and its immediate surroundings. In the one which he painted in 1809, the house can just been seen peeping through the woodland *(See colour section)*.

Those painted in 1811 are referred to by Iolo Williams in his *Early English Watercolours*. He describes them as 'an extremely pleasing group of drawings', chiefly studies of trees in parkland, though one was clearly of the house itself:[22]

> 'One especially delicious example, rather different from the others,
> is a perspective along a classical colonnade outside a house, at the
> end of which a lady in white holds up a small child in her arms,
> while a brown dog lies by the house door. All looks sunny and fine,
> but a note on the back tells us that there is thunder about'.

One of Newbery's sons, William, also became an amateur painter, studying at Oxford under J.B. Malchair, a friend of Crotch and like him a musician as well as an artist of considerable repute. John Newbery was also a friend of John Constable. And, to add to the Newberys' artistic connections, both he and his wife also had their portraits painted by one of the most renowned practitioners of the day of that art – George Romney.

So it was a very distinguished and diversified artistic circle – including leading writers, musicians and painters of the times – to which the Newberys belonged. We do not know how many more of their friends came down to the Park, but it is easy to imagine that the house frequently echoed to the strains of the music which Newbery so much loved, as well as to his own playing of the violin. No doubt too the poems, novels, and essays of the day were eagerly read and discussed. Though it was wartime, and there was much misery beyond the gates, Heathfield Park for Newbery and his family was an oasis of cultured pleasures as well as frequent fun.[23]

TURNER'S 'VALE OF HEATHFIELD'

Around the time that the war came to an end, Heathfield Park had a visit from one of the most distinguished of all British painters - William Turner. He came to execute a commission on behalf of 'Jolly Jack' Fuller of Rosehill, Brightling.

Some years earlier, in 1810 when Turner at the age of 35 was already generally recognised as the leading British landscape and marine painter, Fuller had asked him to paint four watercolours of the area covered by the Sussex constituency for which he was a Tory Member of Parliament. Turner was paid the huge sum for the times of 100 guineas just for the hire of the resulting works so that Fuller could make prints of them to present to his neighbours and friends - though eventually he bought all four. He was not at all put out by the fact that Turner, in his usual niggardly way, having been asked to breakfast when he had delivered one of his paintings had subsequently returned to demand three shillings for his cab fare.[24]

In about 1815 Turner undertook a further series of views of places of interest in east Sussex, including Heathfield Park. He made it the centrepiece of a wide panorama looking south towards the Downs and the sea. He was now at the height of his powers: the result was a large and impressive watercolour - *The Vale of Heathfield*. It offers a wide-angled south-facing panorama looking down across the park towards the sea, its mansion surrounded by a great swirl of woodland, with Heathfield church visible in the middle distance. On the extreme right of the picture is the Gibraltar Tower shown in a very elevated position, while in the foreground is a stretch of heathland. This area is painted in a mainly sandy colour, the trees in subtle blends of green and grey, while in the middle distance a smokey blue predominates *(See colour section)*.[25]

Turner's treatment of the subject and the spirit of his painting are in quite sharp contrast with Repton's drawings some twenty years earlier. Their purposes were, of course, different but it is very striking that Turner was much less concerned with accurate representation (both the depiction of the mansion and the positioning of the tower are clear cases in point) than with the overall pictorial effect. And while Repton's watercolours are still very classical in their design and execution Turner's expresses a clearly romantic view of the natural world.

The painting - which is now housed in the British Museum - was also made into a print, as was the fashion at the time. Fuller provided the finance for the line-drawing of both this and others in what was intended to be a three-volume set of prints with the title *Views in Sussex*. The series itself never

THE HEATHFIELD ESTATE,

IN SUSSEX,

Distant from London, 51 miles; from Brighton, 23; from Hastings, 19; from Tunbridge Wells, 14; and from Eastbourne, 15.

To be Sold by Private Contract.

Applications to be made to Messrs. TYRRELL and SON, Guildhall, London; or to Messrs. HOPER and SONS, Lewes; where Maps of the Estate may be seen.

THE ESTATE

CONSISTS OF AN ELEGANT AND SUBSTANTIAL

Mansion,

Late the Property and Residence of FRANCIS NEWBERY, Esq. deceased, and formerly of LORD HEATHFIELD:

AN ANCIENT PARK,

Three miles and a half in circumference, comprised in a grant of Park and Free Warren from King James the 1st.

The Manor of Broomham,

And several valuable FARMS, containing in the whole 2083A. 2R. 4P. of Arable, Meadow, Pasture, Wood Land, and Hop Ground, lying very compactly, with suitable Farm Houses, Cottages, and Outbuildings, in good repair, in the Parishes of Heathfield, Burwash, and Waldron, in the County of Sussex.

The MANSION is beautifully situated on a commanding eminence in the Park, its Southern front is ornamented with a Corinthian Colonnade 60 feet by 19, and it contains,

ON THE GROUND FLOOR,

An elegant Suite of Apartments, consisting of a Dining Room, 33 feet by 24, and 16½ high; Drawing Room, 24 feet square; Breakfast Room, 22 feet by 17; and Gentleman's Dressing Room;

ABOVE,

Five excellent Bed Chambers on the first floor, and good Attics.

The Interior Domestic Offices,

In the Basement, consist of a spacious Kitchen, Housekeeper's Room, Butler's Pantry, and Servants' Hall, with their appropriate Appendages, and ample Cellars.

The Detached Offices,

Comprise a spacious Riding House, Stables for 16 Horses and a large loose Stable, Coach Houses, Ice House, Game-keeper's House and Kennels, Wash-house, Brew-house, Laundry, and all other requisite Buildings.

Within the Park are large walled Gardens, a fine succession of well stocked Fish Ponds, a handsome Lodge of Entrance, and an ornamental Stone Tower 59 feet high, commanding extensive views of the Sea, the South Downs, and the surrounding Country.

The Park itself is richly wooded; its Scenery is most beautiful, and the Prospects from all parts of it are delightfully varied and extensive; it is stocked with Deer; and there is no Public Way over any part of it.

Without the Park Palings, but near the Mansion, are Cottages for Gardeners, and other convenient Residences for married Servants and Workmen; and there is a Water Mill on the Mill Farm.

THE FARMS ARE OCCUPIED BY RESPECTABLE TENANTS.

The WOODS and PLANTATIONS

Are well stocked with fine, thriving Timber, to the growth of which the Soil is peculiarly congenial.

GAME

Abounds on the whole Estate; excellent Lime Stone for agricultural and architectural Purposes is dug on various parts; also Sandstone for building.

The Land Tax has been redeemed, and the Woods are Tythe-free.

—◇—

Printed by LEE, Lewes.

Sale particulars, 1819

ESRO ACC 5281/962

materialised but a print of *The Vale of Heathfield* was published by Murray and Cooke on 1 March 1819, and was also included in a volume of views of Sussex published the following year.[26]

To judge by the number of copies of this print – as well as the variations of it – which are still in circulation, a considerable quantity must have been produced. And although it does much less than justice to Turner's painting, and the colours (applied by hand individually to each copy after it was printed) are often far removed from those of the original, it certainly brought Heathfield Park to the attention of a much wider public than ever before, and confirmed the national prominence the estate had now acquired. These prints together with the original watercolour also provide a lasting record of the the Park and its magnificent setting, and are a fitting tribute to Newbery's period of ownership.

END OF THE NEWBERY ERA

Although he must have been delighted at this recognition of Heathfield Park, Newbery's later years there were not a time of unalloyed delight. There were also, as in every family, times of sorrow. In January 1804 his eldest daughter, Mary, died at the age of 33 and in August the following year both his second son, Robert, and Charlotte, his youngest daughter, were also struck down. These losses must have cast a long shadow over the Newberys' later years at the Park, which for the country at large were also years of hard struggle against the French under Napoleon.

Francis Newbery himself lived long enough, no doubt fortified by the good air of Heathfield, to see the end of the war which followed on the defeat of Napoleon at Waterloo in June 1815. He was 75 when he died three years later at his London house on 7 August 1818. He was buried in All Saints' Heathfield in the vault originally intended for Lord Heathfield. A plaque on the south side of the choir lists also the other members of the Newbery family laid to rest in the vault. They include his wife Mary, who may have been at least in part responsible for another new feature of the Heathfield scene, the National School (or 'Round School' from its shape), which was built by public subscription and opened in November 1819. Mrs Newbery survived her husband by more than ten years, reaching the age of 82 before her death on 31 January 1829.[27]

8. THE IMPERIAL CONNECTION : THE BLUNTS (1819–1890)

Following the death of Francis Newbery, the Park and its estate – now extending to just over two thousand acres – was put on the market by his trustees early in 1819, and bought in September that year by Sir Charles Richard Blunt Bt. This began a connection with the Blunt family which lasted for over seventy years into the closing decade of the 19th century – and was to be briefly renewed later by another member of the same family after the second world war.

FAMILY BACKGROUND: THE SOUTH SEA BUBBLE

There are several different families bearing the name of Blunt, a number of whose members have at various times achieved fame and/or notoriety. This was certainly true of John Blunt, the great-grandfather of the first member of the branch of the family to own Heathfield Park, and the first member of it to become a baronet. He was a very controversial figure who had to abandon his chosen career in public disgrace – though he managed to hang on to a considerable part of the fortune he had earlier acquired.

John Blunt rose to fame and acquired his fortune as a leading London financier in the early 18th century. A Baptist, he was born in Rochester, Kent, the son of a prosperous shoemaker. Described as 'burly and overbearing, glib, ingenious and determined to get on', he made straight for the City where he soon developed an expertise in financial management, and in 1710 was appointed an adviser to the Tory Chancellor of the Exchequer, Robert Harley. He became responsible for the organisation of the first state lottery in Britain – a device for extracting money from the public whose attractions have only recently been rediscovered in this country.[1]

Sir John Blunt, 1st Bt

It was at this time that he began the family's connection with the East India Company, of which he was briefly a Director in 1710–11. Shortly afterwards, that connection – and his own finances – were reinforced by a second marriage to a wealthy and well-connected lady whose father had worked for the East India Company and become Governor of Bengal. But though this imperial connection was to prove very important for the family in the future, it was John Blunt's subsequent involvement in the South Sea Company which brought him public prominence, and notoriety.

Blunt took a leading part in the setting up and promotion of the Company which was an ingenious device by which the Tory government of the day sought to reduce the burden of the new national debt by privatising it. Those who had lent money to the government were offered shares in the company, which was given a monopoly of trade with south America, in exchange for their government securities, with the expectation of a much higher annual return and a potential capital gain. It appeared to be a certain winner for everyone involved.

Once approved by Parliament in April 1720 investors piled in, and fuelled by euphoria about its future profits, the price of shares in the company soared. In June George I bestowed a baronetcy on Blunt 'for his extraordinary services in raising the public credit'. Plans were announced for a grand 'South Sea Square' to be built on the site of what is now St James's Park underground station.

But in September confidence faltered and then collapsed among rumours of market-rigging and corruption in high places. The bubble had burst. In little more than a fortnight Blunt sank 'from being the most courted to being the most despised and hated man in London'. A parliamentary committee of enquiry was set up, which led in January 1721 to his arrest, together with other directors and staff. It was the end of Blunt's career. He retired to Bath to spend the last fourteen years of his life in comparative obscurity. But although he had to forfeit all except £5000 of the money he had made out of the company, he held on to the rest, and left over £184,000 when he died in 1733.[2]

THE IMPERIAL CONNECTION

In the meantime Blunt had placed his eldest son, John, with the East India Company and it was this connection which was to ensure the continued financial prosperity of several successive generations of the family. The company had been founded in 1600 and been granted a monopoly of trade with India. But the need to protect its trading posts and its commercial interests, not least against rival Dutch and French companies, led it into a growing political and military involvement. In 1757 Robert Clive's victory at Plassey over the 55,000-strong army of the Nawab of Bengal led to the virtual annexation of that state. From then on, in the wake of the collapse of the Mogul empire which left a power-vacuum in the rest of the conti-nent, the East India Company became the means by which British imper-ial rule over India was gradually established.

Although working for the company in Bengal was always regarded as risky for the health, it was also a good way to make a fortune. In addition to a regular salary, there were many opportunities for making money on the side. So entry into the service, which required nomination by one of the Directors, was much sought after. It was also jealously protected: the hered-itary principle prevailed, and there was a good deal of intermarriage between Company families. Young men were recruited at an early age: the first rung on the ladder was as a 'writer' which normally occupied five years. Beyond that lay a hierarchy of factor, junior merchant, and eventually senior merchant. The aim of most who worked for the company was to make enough money as soon as possible so they could retire home and live in style as country gentlemen.[3]

It was through this route, and with this ambition, that Sir Charles Richard Blunt arrived at Heathfield Park. His father, the third baronet, had spent twenty years working for the East India Company. After leaving a wife and numerous family in England 'in very slender circumstances' he soon obtained 'a lucrative appointment in the bullock contract, besides a share in the post office, and forming honourable and advantageous connexions, he married his daughters to men of family, fortune and merit'. He rose to the rank of Postmaster General in Bengal and had accu-mulated £100,000 by the time of his death there in August 1802. Three-quarters of this fortune was left to his eldest son.[4]

Sir Charles William Blunt, 3rd Bt

The beneficiary, Charles Richard Blunt, who now became the 4th baronet, was born on 6 December 1775, and had joined the East India Company as a writer at the age of seventeen, arriv-ing in Bengal late in 1794. He rose rapidly through

Extract from deeds of sale, 1819

a series of posts and was promoted in 1802 – it was said at the time 'on account of his merit and eminent services' – to the important and prestigious post of tax collector of Dacca at a handsome salary of £4000 a year. He subsequently moved over to the judiciary, becoming a judge and magistrate at Beerbhoom and Hooghly and then officiating judge of the provincial court of Calcutta in 1810. After seventeen successful years in Bengal he was able to retire at the age of 35 and return to England in 1811, ready for a new style of life.[5]

It was, however, eight years before he alighted on Heathfield Park. Negotiations began in the Spring of 1819 and a preliminary agreement was reached in early June that year on a price of £47,500 pending confirmation of titles and a valuation of the timber and underwood. This was followed by an agreement in August that the purchaser should be allowed to take possession once he had paid a deposit of £20,000. This Sir Charles did on 3 September – but it then took over a year for agreement to be reached on a price for the timber and underwood and other outstanding matters.

Newbery's trustees – his three surviving sons, John, Charles and William – had already been irritated by Blunt's reversal of his original decision to purchase the furniture in the mansion. An increasingly acrimonious correspon-

dence passed between George Hoper of Hoper and
Sons of Lewes acting for the estate and Blunt's solicitor. At one stage the Newberys threatened to take
the matter to court, but wiser councils prevailed:
agreement was eventually reached in June 1820
on a price of £10,378.3s0d for the timber on
the estate and at the end of August on
£1215.9s0d for the underwood in the Park
itself. But bickering about a small item of £60
for the steps of the Half Moon Inn, and who
should pay the stamp duty, continued into
September. In the end Sir Charles paid a total of
£68,951.12s10d for the estate: this considerable sum
including a year's interest on the disputed items.[6]

Sir Charles Richard Blunt, 4th
Bt as a young man

Sir Charles was in his early forties when he arrived
at Heathfield Park, and still a bachelor. He set about
improving the mansion, is said to 'have adorned its interior with a valuable collection of paintings', and in 1824 at the age of 48
found himself a wife. She was Sophia, daughter of Richard Baker, M.D. and
the widow of another man who had also served in the East India Company,
Richard Auchmuty. They were married in March: just two years later they
had a son, Walter – their first and only child.

During his time at the Park Sir Charles substantially enlarged the estate
by further purchases which brought it to nearly three thousand acres. He
also diverted a stretch of the road which at that time ran immediately around
the Park onto its present course, leaving the old Half Moon Inn stranded in
between. (Its owner, George Haffenden, built another inn of the same name
in 1843 on the site of the present Jack Cade pub).

But Blunt's most enduring legacy, still in place today, is the wall girdling
the Park itself. Three and a half miles long, it enclosed an area of some 350
acres. It was built, mainly of local stone, by Michael Mepham Harmer, a
member of a branch of the well-known local family then headed by Jonathan
Harmer, a surveyor who became renowned for his terra-cotta bas-reliefs.
Begun in 1833, the wall took three years to complete. It was by any measure
a considerable and costly undertaking. Clearly it was designed to serve an
important private interest by marking the boundaries of the Park in a more
permanent fashion than the existing wooden fence. But it had a public as
well as a private function - to provide jobs for the local unemployed at a
time of widespread poverty and distress.

The church and part of the wall around the park

RELIEVING POVERTY, 1820-30

Since the end of the Napoleonic wars Sussex, and particularly the Weald, had been going through a prolonged period of severe economic depression. Having lost its earlier industrial base it was now almost entirely dependent on agriculture which had always to contend with poor soils, fragmented holdings most of whose owners lacked the capital for improvement, and poor communications. Once the wartime boom in demand ended, prices and employment fell at a time when the population in the county continued to grow - from 160,000 in 1801 to 260,000 by 1831. At the same time many ex-servicemen swelled the labour-force. A series of bad harvests after 1815 added to the general misery. Already before then over a fifth of the workforce was virtually permanently unemployed. The result was widespread hardship and distress.[7]

The responsibility for mitigating the effects of poverty rested on each individual parish, as it had done since Elizabethan times. Those owning land were obliged to contribute to the cost of poor relief, which could take a number of forms including the apprenticeship of poor children, the provision of materials on which the able-bodied were set to work, and workhouses for the handicapped and destitute. Some topping-up of wages also took place, and this became a common practice in southern counties as a result of the 1795 Poor Relief Act. The level of relief was often related to the price of bread and the number of children in the family, following a precedent set by Berkshire JPs for the village of Speenhamland, the name by which the practice came to be known. By 1801 there were 37,000 regular recipients of poor relief in Sussex, which had the highest poor rates in the whole of England.

Shortly after he arrived at the Park Sir Charles was forcibly reminded of the extent of the problem in Heathfield itself. Like his predecessor he had been appointed a Justice of the Peace, and it was in this capacity that he was asked to chair a meeting on 20 January 1820 to carry out the provisions of a new poor-law Act passed the previous year. The members of 'the Select Vestry' (substantial householders or occupiers, together with the vicar, churchwardens and the Overseers of the Poor) had to consider no less than 150 claims for relief. They were also required to undertake an enquiry into 'the state and condition of the Poor of the Parish' and to 'cheque the growth of pauperism by the exercise of such legal just and salutary measures as may appear practicable and calculated to the attainment of that object'. The Vestry was rather flummoxed by this second requirement. It declared that 'an Evil of such duration can only be expected to yield to measures the result of the most deliberate and mature consideration'. Like all committees confronted with a difficult problem it decided to defer this matter to a future meeting.[8]

In fact the situation continued to worsen and costs continued to rise in spite of the efforts of the parish authorities who were obliged to raise an additional voluntary subscription, as well as squeezing relief payments. In September 1822 these were restricted to workers earning less than nine shillings a week, except for those with more than two children or who fell sick. In 1824, faced by ever-increasing demands, it was decided to take out a £700 bank loan and, shortly afterwards, to recommend to local employers to raise wages to ten shillings a week, hoping in this way to reduce the burden on the parish ratepayers.

As elsewhere in Sussex, more drastic measures were also in preparation. On 23 April 1824 Sir Charles was again called to preside over a meeting, this time of the local landowners to discuss help for a family to emigrate to America. It was agreed to raise up to £200 for this purpose by another voluntary subscription. At the same time, no doubt as a result of some dissatisfaction with the uneven burden of poor rate contributions, it was also agreed that a new valuation of the parish was needed. As this was a delicate and difficult task, it was to be undertaken by a committee of fifteen, chosen by ballot.

By 1830 the situation had grown even worse. In April that year Sir Charles chaired a meeting at the Star Inn of all the ratepayers in the parish to consider a more extensive scheme 'of appourtioning a portion of the paupers of the parish with the means to going to America'. Detailed discussion followed of the type of help to be given (free passage and subsistence, and a sum to live on until they could find a job) and how much should be given to each. In the end twenty-two adults and fourteen children were included in the scheme which, together with overheads, cost £291.7s. Of this, £290 was loaned by Sir Charles. In all, some sixty people emigrated from the parish to America in 1830-31.

But this level of social distress was bound to lead to trouble, and in the autumn of 1830 riots broke out in Kent and by November had spread into Sussex. Known as the 'Captain Swing' riots from the name some of the rioters used, in two months there were 102 separate incidents, two-thirds of them in the eastern half of the county. The most common were acts of arson, setting fire to ricks and barns, threats to landowners, and demands for higher wages.

It was an ugly situation, and on 8 November 1830 Sir Charles took part in a Special Petty Sessions held at the George Inn, Battle to consider 'the best means of defeating the nefarious and diabolical outrages of Incendiaries'. That meeting, however, took a very moderate line, calling on 'all Persons of whatever Rank' to rally to the side of law and order – but also recommending that landowners should 'consult and advise with their parishioners as to the best mode of employing the Labourers at proper and sufficient wages.' The parish authorities in Heathfield took immediate action, meeting the following day at the Star to agree to fund for a further year sixty extra labourers. But elsewhere retribution and repression followed: at a special Winter Assizes in Lewes 52 men and women were tried, one being executed, 17 transported to Australia and 16 jailed.[9]

A REFORMING MP

These experiences no doubt played an important part in shaping Sir Charles's political convictions and in establishing his reputation locally as a man of liberal principles and a reformer. They also fuelled his political ambitions: he had already stood in 1818, 1819 and 1820 as a parliamentary candidate for a Cornish borough in token opposition to well-established patrons. In 1831 a more propitious opportunity presented itself. Following the accession

Heathfield Park – the seat of Sir C R Blunt (c. 1825)

of William IV in 1830 and the subsequent replacement of the Duke of Wellington as prime minister by a Whig administration under Earl Grey, reform was in the air. The overthrow of the autocratic Charles X in France that year and his replacement by a limited monarchy under Louis Philippe also revived interest in constitutional reform. Better that than revolution, it was argued.

Pressure concentrated on reform of the electoral system for parliament with the aim of weakening the grip exercised in many constituencies, and particularly the 'rotten' boroughs, by a small group of landed aristocracy. The affluent middle class now wanted a greater say in the affairs of government. This tide of opinion became vocal in Lewes as elsewhere in the country. In September 1830 a public meeting sent a letter of congratulations to the 'Brave Parisians for their late Glorious Struggle...in opposition...to their late imbecile Ruler', and the following January 263 Lewes residents signed a petition to Parliament in favour of reform. It was at about the same time that Sir Charles was approached to stand as a reform candidate in the general election that was expected to take place very soon. It was a singular honour for someone so lately arrived in the county, and a resident in a relatively remote corner of it. It was also a reflection of the strength of the reform movement that it was confident about fielding such a candidate.[10]

At that time Lewes was represented by two MPs who, as for much of the later part of the 18th century, were at opposite poles of the political spectrum, reflecting a close balance among the town's electors. The reformers were represented by Thomas Read Kemp. He had originally been an MP for the borough between 1811 and 1816 and after an interval as a dissenting preacher had returned to politics and been re-elected in 1826. By that time he had also became a building entrepreneur in Brighton, giving his name to the new development of Kemp Town. The Tory member was Sir John Shelley of Maresfield Park who had angered many local people by supporting Wellington in his opposition to reform.

Sir Charles set out to capture Shelley's seat. He fired off his opening salvo in a letter addressed to 'the Independent Electors' of the borough published in the *Sussex Advertiser* on 28 March 1831:

> 'I lose no time in announcing to you that it is my intention to obey the call, which I have received in a Requisition most respectably and numerously signed, to become a Candidate... whenever a Dissolution of Parliament may take place.
>
> It is proper that I should at the same time make you acquainted with the *Principles* by which my Public Conduct will be regulated by informing you that I most cordially concur in the Measure for Reform proposed by His Majesty's Ministers...
>
> Gentlemen, I declare to you that I abhor corruption in every shape, that I am a Friend to Freedom throughout the world, never forgetting the poor Slave, and that on all occasions you will find me the honest and strenuous Advocate for Retrenchement and Economy'.

The strength of local support for reform was amply demonstrated at a public meeting held at the County Hall in Lewes on Thursday 7 April attended, it was estimated, by nearly four thousand people. Chaired by the High Sheriff, it voted unanimously to send an address in favour of the Reform Bill both to the King and the two Houses of Parliament. Sir John Shelley, who had recently voted against it, had a very rough reception, being greeted with 'great noise and laughter'. His argument that the ultimate result of the Bill would be 'the total destruction of all social order and good government' did not go down at all well. On the other hand Sir Charles was received with three hearty cheers. He likened the Reform Bill to a safety valve on a steam engine – 'without it, a dreadful explosion might be expected'. He added that he resided in a neighbourhood of some 10,000 people, 'and he would be bold to say that not one of the number was opposed to the measure of Reform'.

In the face of such opposition, Shelley chose to withdraw just before the election was held on 29 April, so that occasion was transformed into a victory parade. Sir Charles, accompanied by his wife, was escorted to Lewes 'by almost thirty of the tenantry and other respectable inhabitants of Heathfield, well mounted'. Arriving at Malling Hill at about half past nine in the morning, he was joined by his local supporters including the members of the Bundle of Sticks club waving elegant new blue banners. Four abreast, they processed through the Cliffe and up the High Street 'amidst the loud and reiterated huzzas of the delighted inhabitants'. Sir Charles and his party then took breakfast at the home of Mr Wood, the brewer. In the meantime another procession had met and accompanied Mr Kemp who had arrived from Brighton at the top of the town: his party carried orange banners and favours.

At eleven o'clock the two candidates were escorted to the hustings where some six thousand people had gathered. In his speech Sir Charles again stressed that he was 'a zealous and strenuous advocate for Reform', and not only of the electoral system, but also the system of poor relief and the game laws. He managed to sound both radical and reassuring. For while he declared that 'this is my principle – to take the burthen off the poor man and place it upon the rich, whose broad shoulders are better able to bear it', he also stressed that 'I will advocate every possible retrenchment and economy in every department of the State'.

As there were no other candidates both he and Kemp were declared elected. After lunch the ceremony of Chairing the Members took place, followed by a triumphant procession in carriages through the town escorted by their joyful supporters. Houses in every street were ablaze with orange and blue, tastefully decorated with evergreens, and graced by elegant ladies observing the scene from open windows. The proceedings went on until between four and five in the afternoon, at which point Sir Charles and his party left for Heathfield Park, his tenantry staying behind to be entertained to dinner in Lewes.[11]

A few days later the local paper, commenting on the Whig success at the election, wrote 'Thank heaven the crisis has passed...Reform stands triumphant'. But in fact there was still a long way to go, and several more crises, before the Reform Bill finally reached the statute book in June 1832. Sir Charles supported it all the way – and was duly rewarded by being returned unopposed with Kemp at the general election in December that year. Three years later the two of them also successfully fought off a vigorous Conservative challenge, Sir Charles emerging with by far the greatest number of votes – 511, compared with 382 for Kemp and 359 for their opponent, the Hon. Henry Fitzroy.[12]

In Parliament Blunt was a dutiful but not vociferous Member: he does not appear to have delivered a full speech throughout the nine years he sat at Westminster. Nor was he given governmental preferment. But as a back-bencher he presented a number of petitions; brought in a bill relating to charges on turnpike roads which passed into law; and, true to his opposition to slavery, voted with a minority in favour of its immediate abolition in the colonies. When he had to face the electors of Lewes again in July 1837 he told his supporters in the Bundle of Sticks club that he had backed those measures of the government which he thought would promote the best interests of society, and had opposed the government when he thought differently from them. If re-elected he would pursue the same course.[13]

On this occasion there was a very keen and evenly-fought contest, with the Conservatives again fielding Henry Fitzroy as well as another candidate. At the nomination meeting Sir Charles was received with a mixture of cheers and hisses. He told those gathered outside County Hall that 'He was not so young a man as he was forty years ago, but although his pace might not be so fast, they might rely on this: that he had not lost any of his bottom'. On polling day there was great suspense: when the result was declared Sir Charles again emerged top of the poll with 413 votes, but Fitzroy was close on his heels with 401. Thomas Brand gained 398, and William Lyon 343.[14]

Less than three years later, in March 1840, Sir Charles died at his London home in Eaton Place at the age of sixty-four, a much respected figure. He had established what appeared to be a solid base for the family at the Park. But although Blunts continued in ownership for another fifty years his successors were not destined to enjoy it as he had done.

THE LATER BLUNTS: A TRAGEDY AND AN ABSENTEE

His immediate successor was his son, Walter, who was only thirteen when he inherited the title and the estate in 1840. Unhappily, he was not to enjoy either for very long. The portrait by Alfred Edward Chalon, R.A. painted that year, shows him under the portico at Heathfield Park, a tall, slight and evidently delicate young man.

While he was at school he may have lived with his mother at their London house for at least part of the time: the 1841 census recorded that a Mr George

Portrait of Sir Walter Blunt, 5th Bt by A E Chalon

Money and various members of his family (together with eight servants) were living at the Park, and four years later George Edward Platt was a tenant there.[15]

During this period Lady Sophia kept a close eye on the affairs of the estate: her initials appear on the bailiff's accounts until her son came of age in March 1847. These provide a rare insight into the details of the management of the estate. At this time the bailiff (who was paid £80 a year) was responsible for annual expenditure of around £600 which included the wages of outside labourers; the purchase of building materials, fuel, and fodder; carpentry, painting, plumbing and glazing; thatching; molecatching (at 1s 6d a dozen), the payment of tolls, parish tithes and poor rate, and Sir Walter Blunt's contribution to the Heathfield Penny Clothing Club – which in 1842 amounted to £5.8s 4d representing 4s 4d for each of 25 families. Many local people figure in these account books as providers of goods or services: they include William and Sylvan Harmer, George Haffenden, William Skinner, Edward Weeks, William Gosling, Thomas Uckfield, Edward Long and William Cornwell. [16]

The last two of these were among the suppliers of seedling trees: it is clear that a very active and extensive programme of planting was being carried out. In June 1841 there was a delivery of 4000 seedling larch, 2000 Scotch fir, 1000 Spanish chestnut and 200 spruce, and in October of another 2000 chestnut, 2000 birch, 700 alder, and 600 willow. The following year a further 22,500 seedlings were bought, followed by 15,100 in 1843, over 29,000 in 1845, and in 1846 another 16,200 including 10,000 Spanish chestnut.

But if the estate gave rise to a good deal of expenditure, it also was an important source of revenue. In 1844, according to a note in the accounts, it yielded just over £1600 in rents, out of Lady Blunt's total income of almost £4000. It was in that year Sir Walter went up to Christ Church, Oxford – with an allowance of £500 a year. By then he was already a keen sportsman: he also became an accomplished watercolour artist. He made a number of sketching tours of Devon, Wales and Derbyshire, and continued to paint when he went abroad to the Alps in 1846, having been diagnosed as suffering from tuberculosis.

By early in March 1847 he had returned to live at the Park. He painted his last two watercolours there shortly before his death on 13 July following a riding accident in the Park when his horse plunged while negotiating the steep side of the ghyll. He was buried in the family vault in the cemetery at Heathfield parish church. He had been the owner of the park for only just over seven years. His talent as an artist was not revealed to the public until a hundred and forty years later, when an album of his water-colours was discovered and exhibited at the Swan Gallery, Sherborne in 1987.[17]

The album was compiled by his cousin, Charles William, who in the absence of a direct heir became the sixth baronet. He had been born in Calcutta but was educated at Edinburgh University and Trinity College, Cambridge, and went on to make his living as a barrister in London, for which he qualified in 1835 as a member of the Middle Temple. He was thirty-six when he inherited the Park, unmarried, and destined to remain a bachelor. He had also inherited land and properties elsewhere in Sussex, including Waldron and Ringmer. It is not clear where or to what extent he resided in the county during the rest of his lifetime – but what is certain is that the Mansion in the Park was rented out for a good deal of the time, and probably continuously from the late 1850s until his death in 1890.

Most of the tenants lived in some style – attended, in the manner of the times, by a good number of resident servants. George Edward Towery, who was there at the time of the 1851 Census, was rather modest in this respect: he only had a housekeeper, two housemaids, a dairymaid, groom and cowman. But James Johnson Ellis, who is recorded as being at the Park in 1859 and 1861 and may have spent five or six years there, was in a very different category. He was the son of a well-known and large-scale hop grower of Barming, near Maidstone. He, too, was a man of Kent, having previously lived at the Priory, East Fairleigh. He was reported arriving in late April 1859 with his wife, family "and suite". Two years later the census enumerator, rather baffled (as others have been) by the absence of a name for the mansion which he called the 'Place', recorded that it was occupied not only by a substantial number of members of the Ellis family - four sons, a daughter, a sister-in-law, two nieces and a nephew - but also by ten servants: a governess, cook, kitchen maid, housemaid, an upper- and an under-nursemaid, a butler, indoor boy, and two grooms.[18]

In 1866-7 Frederick Peel Miller, a well-known Surrey cricketer, was living there while the 1871 Census records the presence of a banker, Colonel Charles Wright, together with his wife, son, three daughters, German governess, and nine live-in servants. Three years later Lord Claud Hamilton, later to become an MP for South Kensington, was also a tenant, but proba-bly for only a short period, for in that year Mr Francis Henry Scott took over the tenancy which he was to keep for sixteen years before eventually buying the Park.[19]

Throughout this period Sir Charles William Blunt nevertheless continued to own, manage – and derive income from – the extensive Heathfield Park estate. Edmund Brand, who lived in Portland Square, was his land-steward for 'very many years' (certainly from 1861 and probably much earlier) until he was succeeded on his death in 1886 by his son. Blunt also maintained strong local connections and was active in the life of the county. In his early years as a magistrate he was a regular attender on the Bench at Hailsham petty sessions and also at the East Sussex Quarter Sessions in Lewes. In 1873 he served a term as High Sheriff for the county and also became Deputy Lieutenant.[20]

However, his attempts to emulate his uncle's career as a local Member of Parliament were not successful. Blunt tried twice to get elected for Lewes, most notably in 1859 – but as a Conservative at a time when the Whigs' hold on the town (which his forbear had done so much to establish!) was still very strong. There had been no contested parliamentary election for the past twelve years and even then the Conservatives clearly had difficulty in mounting a challenge. Of their two candidates, Blunt was still a relative newcomer in the county, living up-country, and the other, R.P.Amphlett, was a Q.C without any local connections at all. Blunt tried to widen his appeal by describing himself as a 'liberal-conservative', but was mocked by his opponents for doing so. "What sort of hybrid is this ?" one of them asked. In the event the two Liberal candidates, Henry Fitzroy and Henry Brand were elected by 339 and 338 votes against 200 for Amphlett and 189 for Blunt.

Nevertheless, this result was seen as encouraging by the Conservatives. The vote, said the *Sussex Express* (though not the most unbiased source) 'has animated the Conservative body with the fullest hopes of future success'. Shortly afterwards a public dinner was organised for Blunt and Amphlett in the Corn Exchange. Described by the newspaper as a 'Great Conservative Festival', it was attended by 250 supporters including – it was asserted – 'a very large proportion of the trading and commercial class of Lewes'. In the course of the proceedings it was proposed and agreed that a Conservative Club be founded, and an elegant blue flag bearing the words 'The Lewes Blue Club 1859' was unfurled to general acclaim. So even if Blunt was thwarted in his own political ambitions, there was some satisfaction in the result and the promise it held for the future.[21]

During the remainder of his lifetime, which Blunt increasingly spent in London where he had a house in Warwick Street, just north of Piccadilly, he nevertheless continued to maintain a close interest in local affairs in Sussex. He served as a member of Heathfield school management committee at least from 1861 until 1884, contributing an annual £10 to the school funds, and extra amounts from time to time. In December 1875 he drew attention to the inadequate stipend of the assistant mistress, Mary Ann Brook, and persuaded the committee to agree to 'the propriety of increasing it'. He also continued as a Churchwarden at Heathfield Parish Church into the 1880s, for part of the time sharing with Scott the task of distributing each Christmas relief for the poor of the parish in the shape of one pound of meat for each adult and ½lb for each infant.[22]

MID-VICTORIAN HEATHFIELD

The times were no longer so harsh as in the aftermath of the Napoleonic wars, and from about 1840 to the early 1870s most of the south-east enjoyed a period of comparative prosperity. But in Sussex, where one in six of the labour-force was still employed in agriculture, this was true of the coast and the Downs rather than the Weald, where most farmers were small-scale producers, and poor. There were, however, some important shifts going on in the pattern of agricultural production. There was, for instance, a steady growth in the production of hops in the Heathfield district to meet the rising consumption of beer. This no doubt accounts for the arrival of Mr Ellis and entourage at the Park at the end of the 1850s. The crop was a staple at the weekly market at the Crown Inn, which also dealt in corn and seeds.[23]

From the early 1830s there was also the beginning of an agricultural industry which was to become a notable feature of the Heathfield area for the next hundred years or so. This was based on the artificial fattening of chickens. In the 1851 census a number of higglers appear in the Heathfield area - the middle men who collected the chickens from the producers and sold them on to those who fattened them for market. This last part of the process took three to four weeks, when they were fed on a diet of ground oats, mixed with tallow (rendered-down animal fat) and skimmed milk. The finished products, plucked, singed, and powdered with flour, were packed into wooden crates for transport to the Smithfield market.[24]

There was also evidence of more middle-class money in the district, as well as of Victorian piety, in the extensive rebuilding of the parish church at Heathfield which began in the late 1840s and was only completed twenty years later. Among other things, this involved taking down and reconstructing the 60-foot spire, rebuilding the south chapel, aisle and porch, and removing the organ-loft and gallery. In the process a great deal of the earlier character of the church was lost - but Heathfield was certainly not the only example of this well-intentioned Victorian vandalism.[25]

The new Heathfield station

LATE ARRIVAL OF THE RAILWAY.

The population of the parish of Heathfield had grown from just over 1200 in 1801 to around 2000 in 1871: by then it was a large, if still scattered, village. No great changes were to take place until after the arrival of the railway – and that was very late in coming. One major reason for this was that once again the district found itself in a disputed frontier area – this time the protagonists being two rival railway companies, the London Brighton and South Coast, and the London and South Eastern. The former opened its service between London and Brighton in September 1841, and the following year the South Eastern reached as far as Tonbridge and Ashford on its way to Folkestone (1843) and Dover (1844). The area between, and particularly access to Hastings, gave rise to a long and bitter battle between the two companies.

In 1848 an agreement was reached under which a line south from Tunbridge Wells to Hastings, to be built by the SER, became the effective demarcation between their respective territories. The final section of this line, running through Battle, was opened on 1 February 1852 – but the nearest it came to Heathfield was at Witherenden, a good six miles away. The station was difficult of access, involving a steep descent into the valley of the Rother.

That was a considerable hazard for the transport available at the time, and even by 1870 local carriers provided only a three-times a week service to the station there, which by then had been renamed Ticehurst Road. It was only much later, in the mid 20th century when this Charing Cross-Hastings line was the only one left after Dr Beeching had wielded his axe, that this station (called Stonegate since June 1974) became the main rail link with the capital for the Heathfield area.[26]

It was not until 1880 – almost thirty years after the opening of the Hastings line – that the railway at last arrived at Heathfield itself. The reasons for this lengthy delay are not hard to identify. Apart from the area being right on the edge of the territory served by the London, Brighton and South Coast Railway company, it was only thinly populated, and its terrain was so difficult that it had been avoided as a direct route to the south coast resorts. In the mid 1860s the LBSCR was seriously interested in building a link between Uckfield and Hailsham – two much more important market towns – but even this fell foul of opposition by the SER and in July 1868 the project for an 'Ouse Valley' line was abandoned.[27]

In the end it was only with the greatest reluctance that the LBSCR embarked on the construction of a line between Tunbridge Wells and Eastbourne. It was pressure from the seaside town, backed by the Duke of Devonshire, which proved decisive. Promoters there threatened to do a deal with the rival SER which in the end had to be bought off by being given a share of the proceeds of the new line. As the chairman of the LBSCR explained to his shareholders in 1877:[28]

> 'The directors most reluctantly came to the conclusion that half
> a loaf was better than no bread and it was better to save two
> thirds or three fourths of the Eastbourne traffic than to lose half
> of it'.

When the company began planning the link between Hailsham and Tunbridge Wells, five different routes were explored. The original intention was to provide a station for the Heathfield area just south of Heathfield Park, with the line running north under the middle of the park through a tunnel which would have been almost a mile long. Preliminary borings showed, however, that there was a difficult stratum of rock in the way, and the route was abandoned. The only remaining traces of it are some air-shafts bored at the time, which were first recorded in the Ordnance Survey map of 1875. The line as finally built, authorised by an Act of Parliament of 1876, skirted round the western side of the Park, passing through land belonging to no less that eight different owners along a half-mile stretch south of the tunnel which was to carry the line northwards from Heathfield.[29]

The station itself was located on empty waste land, most of which belonged to the Heathfield Park estate, at the foot of the hill leading up to the Park, and just inside the parish of Waldron. It was a short distance south of the main east-west road between Uckfield and Hurst Green (the present A265), and not far from the junction at Cross in Hand with the north-south route from Tunbridge Wells to Eastbourne (now the A267).

The line from Hailsham to Heathfield opened on 5 April 1880 although at that stage the station buildings were not finished and the connection to Tunbridge Wells was only completed in September. The water needed for the locomotives had at first to be brought a long way by a one-inch pipe from a spring in Heathfield Park: it was only later that a bore-hole was sunk in the station yard.

The 'Cuckoo Line', as it became generally known, was built on the cheap and was a modest affair both in terms of its infrastructure (a single line with passing places) and the service it provided - five trains a day in each direction on weekdays, three on Sundays. The connections to London and Brighton were inconvenient, drawing a complaint from the parish council, and according to the local newspaper the station waiting room was unheated, uncomfortable and draughty. Nevertheless, the railway proved to be the most important agent of change that the Heathfield area had ever experienced.[30]

A vivid picture of what the area looked like when the line was opened, and how its arrival was already beginning to change things, is provided by a contemporary report in the *Sussex Express*. Entitled 'The new Weald of Sussex railway!' it hailed the line as 'a triumph of engineering skill', and described in detail the terrain it traversed. This element of modernity was in sharp contrast to the village area it was to serve. Outside the gates of Heathfield Park there was a little hamlet of cottages (Portland Square), and at Cade Street a small village which, however 'includes the shops for necessaries, the house of the veterinary surgeon, a few private houses, and the Half Moon, reputed to be an excellent hostelry'. There were a few more houses around the Crown, near the junction with the Burwash road. There the reporter found 'an obliging hostess: her Scotch is recommended'. Earlier in his round of the local hostelries he had paid a visit to the Prince of Wales in Hailsham road ,'where a succulent steak is served'. And there he found the first signs of change brought by the railway line - a new road linking it with the station. He also reported that within a few days of the opening of the railway 400 passengers were using it every day.[31]

END OF THE BLUNT SUCCESSION

Ten years later the railway was used to bring the body of Sir Charles William Blunt back to Heathfield after his death at his London house on 5 November 1890. It arrived by the 12.50 train on Monday 10 November accompanied by a number of mourners and a funeral car. The coffin was placed on it and headed the procession to Heathfield church followed by the new baronet, relatives, friends, the tenantry and workmen on the estate, and local residents. There were at least 300 in the church, the coffin later being carried to the family tomb in the churchyard by eight of the estate workers.[32]

In the absence of a direct heir, the succession again passed to a cousin, William Blunt, who became the seventh baronet. Son of a Bengal civil servant, he too had spent almost thirty years of his life there, and had retired to live at East Grinstead. Now aged 64, he decided not to take up the option of purchasing the Blunt estates in Heathfield, Ringmer, Burwash and Waldron even though he could have done so for a very modest £3000. By now the great agricultural depression had settled on the country, rents were falling, and many estates were sliding into debt. He preferred to sell the estate, part of which was auctioned off at the Swan Hotel, Tunbridge Wells, on 7 August the following year. There was a good attendance and brisk bidding for a number of farms and several houses in the village. But by then the Park and its mansion had already been sold to its long-standing tenant, Mr Francis Henry Scott J.P.[33]

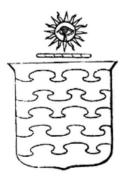

Blunt family coat of arms

Panorama of the new Heathfield

9. HEATHFIELD EXPANDS: THE ESTATE CONTRACTS (1890–1940)

The change in ownership of Heathfield Park in 1890 came at a time when Britain's power and influence in the world were at their peak, its navy supreme, and its industry and colonies a source of steadily-increasing national wealth. For those in the professional middle class who had profited from this, and sought a refuge from town-living, Sussex was one of the areas which beckoned.

Not all of them made for the coast, as the number of substantial and solidly brick-built villas in the Weald dating from this period testify. The tranquillity of the area was one of its great attractions; so, too, was its countryside which many embellished with splendid gardens – including Nymans, Leonardslee, Gravetye, Wakehurst Place and Sheffield Park. The Weald also exerted a great appeal to those in search of artistic or intellectual inspiration. As Chesterton testily complained at the time: 'Short story writers leapt from behind hedges. Minor poets dropped from the trees like ripe fruit. Philosophers, sociologists and artists ran like rabbits about the woods'.[1]

Heathfield Park itself continued to appeal to a rather more traditional clientele. The reduction in the size of its accompanying estate – down from nearly three thousand acres to somewhat under one thousand – and the severing of the long-established link with the Blunt family undoubtedly led to a certain reduction in its standing, confirming a trend which had set in during the long period when it had been rented out. Nevertheless its owners still needed substantial financial resources to buy and maintain it. Of the four who spanned the next fifty years, two had sufficient to live a leisurely country life, making the Park their home, while the other two continued to work in London – though perhaps more through habit and inclination than economic necessity – and used it mainly at weekends and holiday times. None of them had titles and they do not seem to have aspired either to them or to prominent public office. Two became magistrates and sat on the local Bench: all of them became patrons and supporters of a range of local voluntary organisations (including the Conservative party) – but otherwise were content to live essentially private lives.

THE NEW TOWN: HEATHFIELD TOWER

By the time of the change of ownership of the Park in 1890, the railway was beginning to have a profound effect on Heathfield itself. In the first place, by providing much swifter access to the London markets, it gave a big boost to the local poultry rearing and fattening industry. In its opening year Heathfield station handled £60,000 worth of dead poultry: by 1894 this had risen to £140,000, amounting to some 1,300,000 chickens a year. This industry also brought the expansion of others which served it – corn and seed merchants, dairies which sold milk to bind the cram together, butchers who provided the tallow, and so on.[2]

The railway also provided a boost to horticulture in the district – and accidentally led to the discovery of natural gas. This was found in 1896 in the stable yard of the Station Hotel when it was decided to deepen a bore-hole which had been sunk to provide water for the locomotives. The gas was soon being used to provide light for the station, and in 1902 the Natural Gas Fields of England company was set up to exploit it. The supply, however, never matched up to expectations, and two years later the company went into liquidation. Parts of Heathfield continued to be lit by natural gas until 1930 – though fishtail burners had to be used, as ordinary mantles were blown to pieces by the

Preparing chickens for market

Natural gas balloons

pressure – but the town failed to develop a significant industrial base. Nevertheless, more people were drawn into the area: in the thirty years between 1881 and 1911 the population of the parish of Heathfield rose from a little under two thousand to 3150.[3]

Much of the land on which the new urban settlement developed had previously belonged to the Heathfield Park estate: this was now going cheap as a result of the Blunt sale and depressed land values. Initially most of the new houses and shops were located between the Park and the railway along and around the old Hailsham road, down the new road linking this with the station, and around the station itself. It was only later that the new settlement spread to and along the old-established east–west road from Cross in Hand. When the railway arrived there were only two buildings along this stretch of road, but it was nevertheless a much busier route than that to Hailsham, and it was no doubt inevitable that it would eventually become the High Street of the new settlement.

It was only gradually, however, that this happened. At first much of the new activity was focused in and around the station itself - where carriers and grain and coal merchants rapidly established themselves. It then spread with the building of a Station Hotel close by and the first shops in Station Road in the mid 1890s, a Drill Hall in 1897, and four cottages for railway staff in 1899. In the meantime, land on the north side of the main road (then called Tilsmore Road) had become available from the Isenhurst estate, and shops also began to appear there from the mid 1890s. By 1905 this was beginning to be called the High Street, and in the following years a first parade of shops was also built on its south side on land once belonging to Heathfield Park which was put on the market in 1907 by the Tilsmore estate.[4]

*'Heathfield Tower' postmark
1906*

Initially, there was some uncertainty about the name to be given to this new urban settlement. It was nowhere in particular, on a green-field site between Heathfield and Cross in Hand straddling two parishes - Heathfield and Waldron. The station itself was known as 'Heathfield and Cross in Hand'; the area around it as 'Station District'; and the new post office as 'Station Road'. But in 1899, faced by increasing local objections to this postal address, the Head Postmaster at Eastbourne wrote to Heathfield Parish Council asking them to suggest a different name. Unanimously, they suggested 'Tower' Post Office, a reference to Gibraltar Tower in the Park which overlooked the new town. 'Heathfield Tower' was then adopted as not only the postal but also the telegraphic and telephone address for the new Heathfield. It was generally known by this name for the next thirty-five years.[5]

Uncertainty about its name was only one of a number of handicaps from which the new settlement suffered. Like many other new railway towns it lacked an historic centre to give it shape or distinction, and it grew in a piece-meal fashion without any guiding overall plan. It also paid a penalty for straddling two different parishes. When in 1894 parish councils were set up, its affairs were divided between the two - and they in turn became part of two different Rural District Councils, one based in Hailsham, the other in Uckfield.

This divided responsibility (which lasted until 1933 when Waldron was transferred to Hailsham RDC) meant that for almost forty years there was no way in which the needs and interests of the new Heathfield could be properly expressed or met by the new system of local government. Heathfield parish council protested that it was under-represented on the rural district council, and its needs neglected: it constantly complained, for instance, about the neglected state of the local roads, but met with little response.[6]

The new settlement also suffered from the fact that it was a mainly working- and lower middle-class community consisting of tradesmen, shop-keepers and artisans. It lacked a strong middle class professional element which would have given it greater clout in seeking greater public resources to develop its infrastructure. Nevertheless, it did soon begin to develop a charac-ter and life of its own. One important element in this was the continuing strength of the local Nonconformist tradition. It was significant that the prime site in the centre of the new town at the junction of Station Road and High Street was occupied at an early stage by a new Union Church, completed in 1901, financed and run by agreement between local Baptists and Congregationalists (as it still is today). If the established church reigned in the older part of Heathfield, Nonconformity had raised its flag over Heathfield Tower. The Anglicans, for their part, were much slower to react to change: fundraising for a new church only began in 1907 and it was 1912 before St Richards was built as an outpost of the parish church – and then on a site rather peripheral to the main area of the new town.[7]

The Union Church and the High Street, c.1905

The development of the new Heathfield was to have important consequences later on for Heathfield Park and its owners. They, however, had very
little to do with it. The land on which it grew up was no longer theirs, and
they took no part in any of the new local government bodies established at the
end of the 19th century at county, district and parish level. They continued to
live in a sort of island within the walls of the Park, though their links with the
surrounding community did now begin to develop. Like their predecessors,
they provided employment for a good number of local people, and patronised
local shops and services. In addition, they began to open up some new points
of contact with the local community: these were limited in scope, but sugges-
tive of a subtle change in the relationship between the two worlds.

FRANCIS HENRY SCOTT

Some moves in this direction were made by the first owner to follow the
Blunts, Francis Henry Scott JP. He was the son of a Tunbridge Wells family
and was no stranger to Heathfield: he had been a tenant at the Park since 1874,
the year of his marriage at the age of thirty-five. He had been educated
privately, and then at Trinity College, Cambridge and was evidently a man of
means for although he was called to the Bar as a member of Lincoln's Inn, he
subsequently practised for only a short time as a barrister.[8]

Scott's legal expertise was put to good use when he became a Justice of the
Peace in 1881 and he sat regularly on the Hailsham bench. He was also active
in local politics becoming chairman of the local (Eastbourne) Conservative
Association. The *Sussex Express* recorded him chairing a meeting in November
1890 held at the National School in Heathfield, and well attended in spite of a
snowstorm. The speaker was the local Member of Parliament, Admiral Field. He
gave an 'able and lengthy' address, at the conclusion of which Scott implored the
voters of the Division at the next election 'to remember to preserve intact the
national flag and the union of the British Islands'. In due course his work as a
pillar of the local establishment was rewarded by his appointment as a Deputy
Lieutenant of Sussex, a position which he held till his death.[9]

Scott was also a keen sportsman. He was particularly noted for his skill
in driving a four-in-hand coach; he kept a pack of beagles, and organised
and played in his own cricket team. At the same time he also showed 'very
great liberality' to the local village team. He allowed it to play on the ground
in the Park, made handsome donations to its funds, and turned out for it
himself. Already in 1883 it renamed itself 'Heathfield Park Cricket Club' in
grateful recognition. But this was only one instance of his involvement in

local groups and their activities. He and his wife were also responsible for initiating in August 1891, during their first year as owners of the Park, what was to become a notable annual event: a flower and vegetable show held in the grounds in cooperation with the Heathfield Amateur and Cottage Garden Mutual Improvement Society – the fore-runner of the present Horticultural Society.

It was the first opportunity that most local people had had of visiting the Park, and they flocked there from all around, including Brightling, Burwash, Dallington, Mayfield, Rotherfield, Warbleton and Waldron. The *Sussex Express* reported 'that all of the *elite* of the neighbourhood, with scarcely an exception, were present'. The show opened at 2pm, and it was soon evident that 'as far as the attendance of the public was concerned, success was assured'. A good sum – £15.18s10d– was taken at the gates, and a sale of goods in aid of Heathfield National Schools yielded over £83. A 'capital selection of music' was played by the Battle band; the fruit and produce on show was judged by William Bean (Crown Nursery), Mr Thompson (Warbleton Nurseries) and Mr Sievewright (gardener to Lady Neville). Mrs Scott presented the prizes: her husband replied to the vote of thanks on her behalf.[10]

So successful was the occasion that it promptly became an annual fixture. In August 1892, special exhibits *hors concours* were mounted to show off the produce of some other local gardens: Edward Hollman, gardener to Lt-General Dyneley, showed 'some very fine peaches and melons'; Mr Masson, gardener to Mr Logie-Pirie (Tottingworth) exhibited grapes; and William Bean (Tower Nurseries) 'a collection of flowers and pot plans which extended all round one end of the tent and included dahlias, roses and other flowers in a high state of perfection'. The occasion, aided by beautiful weather, was again pronounced an unqualified success. But like all such events out of doors during an English summer, it was not always so fortunate. In 1894, for instance, the weather was 'most unfavourable, the rain falling until about six o'clock in the evening': on that day few braved the elements.

This was the last show held under the auspices of Scott: the following year he moved to Brightling Park where he was to remain for most of the rest of his life. It may be that his wife preferred it – though she died after they had been there only five years. At all events Scott, having married for a second time (to a widow of a Bombay civil servant), but remaining childless, clearly retained a fond memory for Heathfield Park for in February 1917, by then in failing health, he returned as a tenant. It was there he died on 9 September 1918 at the age of 79, described in the *Sussex Express* as 'a real country gentleman and an erstwhile sportsman of the good old English type'.

Portrait of W C Alexander
by Philip Connard

WILLIAM CLEVERLY ALEXANDER

During the intervening years Heathfield Park was owned by William Cleverly Alexander, a successful City man of Quaker origins, who had an extensive family, a fine house in Kensington, and a keen interest in the arts.

Born in April 1840, Alexander spent most if not all of his professional life in the family firm of bill-brokers and bankers, which had offices in Lombard Street, and was well-known in the City. He became chairman of it in 1901, on the death of a brother, and in due course the oldest member of the Discount Market. It was a somewhat risky type of business but one out of which good profits were made. Alexander was able to live in style in Aubrey House on Campden Hill, Kensington; bring up a family of seven children (one son and six daughters); and at the same time collect paintings and become a patron of the arts.[11]

He was still a young man in his early thirties when he befriended the young American painter James McNeill Whistler who had arrived in London in 1859. Alexander commissioned him to paint portraits of his children. One of them, 'Harmony in Grey and Green: Miss Cicely Alexander' took two years and over seventy sittings to complete, and aroused intense controversy when it was first exhibited in 1874, and again in 1881. The sitter was only six years old when the work was begun, and she was frequently reduced to tears by Whistler's relentless search for perfection – he would regularly scrape the whole canvas bare and start all over again. Her misery is clearly apparent in the completed canvas which scandalised many viewers by breaking with the conventional view of little girls as carefree and pretty. But it is a striking and accomplished work which has stood the test of time – as was apparent when it was included in the Whistler exhibition shown at the Tate Gallery in 1994.[12]

Whistler portrait of Cicely Alexander

Alexander was in his mid-fifties when he bought Heathfield Park from Scott in 1895. His wife, Rachel Agnes Lucas, whom he had married in 1861 when he was only 21, had local connections, her parents having lived at Wellingham House, Ringmer. This may well have influenced their choice of a country seat. Like so many owners, before and since, Alexander set about rebuilding and modernising the house. Perhaps by now his tastes had become rather more conventional: at all events the architect he chose, Reginald Blomfield, had revolted against the Arts and Crafts movement in which he had received his initial training, and had become a fierce critic of modern architecture, and a partisan of English classicism. He was already set on a course which was to make him one of the most notable British architects of his time, designing large classic structures including the rebuilding of the Quadrant in Regent Street, part of Piccadilly Circus, and the main gate of the war memorial at Ypres.[13]

The external appearance of the house today is very largely the work of Blomfield, carried out during 1896-7. While respecting the spirit of the original building, he undertook a series of major alterations, including the addition of a new south-east wing, and a new attic storey (the floors there still have the slope of the original roof). He also gave the house new elevations, including a big segmental pediment on the south-facing side, slightly repositioned and

Eastbourne Hunt meet at the Park, c. 1905

rebuilt the veranda, replaced the old slates on the roof by tiles, and stripped the exterior of its stucco to restore the original brickwork and reveal the old stone string courses, aprons and quoins.[14]

Alexander plunged into his new life in the country with enthusiasm. Later to be described as 'a typical country squire' he took to wood-cutting which soon became his favourite hobby, and he and his wife - in spite of their Quaker backgrounds - became great supporters of the local church, to whose funds they made notable contributions. At the same time he and his family took an active part in more secular local activities. The annual shows begun by Scott were continued and by 1906 were being held on August Bank Holiday

From a visitor to the Park, 1905

Monday in cooperation with the Heathfield and District Horticultural Society. Sited close to the Gibraltar Tower (which was also open to the public), the show that year was again very successful. The local paper reported that 'Heathfield's excellent brass band discoursed pleasant music during the afternoon and Professor Zeidler gave a ventriloquial entertainment'.

The following year it rained and attendance was down, but in 1908 the show was blessed with lovely weather, and 'eclipsed all previous efforts on the part of the society'. On that occasion, in addition to the usual attractions of swings, coconut shies, and Mrs Alexander's exhibition of bric-a-brac in the Tower, Heathfield National School's Minstrel Troupe gave a couple of performances that provided 'ample proof that Mr J.E.Smart, the headmaster, had spared no pains in training the boys'; Mr Edwards of Buxted gave 'some very pleasing phonograph selections'; and the Heathfield brass band not only played selections during the afternoon but also provided music for dancing in the evening.

The Alexanders also kept up with changing times: on another occasion they opened the Park for a Motor Gymkhana and Fete. This was a big affair in aid of the Heathfield and Waldron Nursing Association. It began at 11.30 in the morning and went on into the evening, attracting some 1500 visitors. There were events for motor vehicles (including musical chairs) in the paddock on the western side of the mansion for which the music was provided by the Heathfield brass band, and for cycles on the east lawns where the Tunbridge Wells Royal Military Band performed. Among the numerous other attractions, there was a an exhibition of Sussex antiquities in the mansion itself, a market for fruit, flowers and country produce, displays of flag drill and maypole dances by the scholars of the Union Church Sunday school, Morris dances performed by a party of girls, and four performances of humorous songs and musical sketches by Mr Herbert Schartau in the hall. As dusk fell, the proceedings were concluded by a torchlight performance by the Five Ashes Amateur Dramatic Society.[15]

Like the Newberys before them, the Alexanders also put on a Christmas entertainment. On one occasion this consisted of two fairy plays, 'The Golden Goose' and 'Rumpelstiltskin', the parts being played by three of the Alexander daughters, house guests, and local ladies. The proceeds went this time to the Sussex County Nursing Association.[16]

Throughout Alexander's period of ownership, he maintained his London residence, and regularly attended his office in the City. Members of his family travelled back and forth, sometimes by train: on Wednesday 1 September 1897 one of his daughters had a narrow escape in the worst accident that was ever to befall the Cuckoo line. As the 8.55am from Heathfield to Tunbridge Wells was approaching Mayfield on an elevated section of the line the locomotive left the track, and together with the leading coach, fell over on its side, the remaining five coaches crashing down to the bottom of the bank. The engine driver was killed, and thirty out of the forty passengers injured. Miss Alexander 'who showed great spirit under painful circumstances' escaped by climbing through the lamp hole at the top of the carriage in which she was travelling, and though much bruised managed to walk home without help.[17]

Although his wife died in 1900, Alexander had become very attached to the Park and continued to take part in, and support, local activities. He also turned his attention to recording its past, commissioning a young nephew, Perceval Lucas, to compile a history of the Park and the parish of Heathfield. Based in part on a manuscript researched and written in 1821-31 by Sylvan Harmer, this was published in 1910 under the title *Heathfield Memorials*. E.V Lucas, the well-known writer (and brother of Perceval) contributed an introduction, and Alexander himself a number of elegant drawings as illustrations.

Alexander was also an active collector of artefacts from the past, including some fragments of Roman pottery found locally, Wealden firebacks, and a large number of Jonathan Harmer's terra-cotta vases and plaques – a complete set of which he later gave to the Sussex Archeological Society, of which he was a firm supporter.

By the outbreak of the first world war, Alexander was into his seventies. With typical generosity he contributed thousands of pounds to the Red Cross, YMCA and other war charities. In April 1916 he came down to Heathfield on Maundy Thursday to attend the Cuckoo Fair and decided to extend his stay over Easter, selling some bullocks at a record price at

Cuckoo Line accident, 1897

Satinstown Fair, and visiting a married daughter and son-in-law at Horsmonden, from which they returned him in their car on Easter Sunday. After tea and a walk he attended evening service at Heathfield Parish Church, and then had dinner alone in the house. At twenty to ten that evening he said goodnight to his butler Herbert Thomas who then retired to bed in the basement.

Some forty minutes later the butler was aroused by a noise and groans, and discovered his employer – whom he had served for twenty years – lying unconscious on his back at the foot of the back stairs. A local doctor was summoned, as well as two surgeons from London, but Alexander died some three hours later, without regaining consciousness, early in the morning of Easter Monday, 17 April.

A verdict of accidental death was recorded at the subsequent inquest, which was followed by a funeral service at the parish church. The coffin was conveyed there from the mansion on a farm wagon, and then carried by eight estate workers. Many others who had worked for Alexander joined members of the family, friends and local residents for the service before the burial in the churchyard, next to his wife, in a grave lined with ivy from the Park. They also insisted, in spite of the family's wishes, on a floral tribute: it came 'With respectful sympathy to our dear friend and master, from the household and employees of the estate'. The following Sunday the bells of the church were half-muffled as a quarter-peal of Grandsire Doubles and touches of other methods were rung to commemorate Alexander.[18]

It was a farewell to an owner of Heathfield Park in a manner and spirit which was to be repeated only once more – and that quite soon. Alexander was followed at the Park briefly by one of his married daughters, Mrs Grace Lister, who shared with his other children his estate amounting to close on £406,000. But in February 1917 she rented the mansion out to the former owner, Scott, now aged 78. This was, however, to be only a brief coda to the twenty-one years he had already spent at the Park: he died in September the following year. As with Alexander, the funeral service and burial were held at the parish church. Estate workers carried his coffin in a procession which also included, in addition to the family, the local Volunteers and Cadets, Boy Scouts and Wolf Cubs, and servicemen of the Royal Defence Corps, as well as local tradespeople.

These deaths of two successive owners of the Park, who between them had lived there for over forty years, signalled the end of another phase in its history – and one which coincided closely with the end of the first world war, two months later.

THE INTER-WAR YEARS AT HEATHFIELD.

The ending of the war in 1918 was greeted in Heathfield as elsewhere with great relief. The early patriotic fervour had quickly waned as casualty lists lengthened. There were some lighter moments locally when the 'Heathfield Flappers' and the 'Scarlet Runners' gave concerts in aid of the Soldiers' Cigarette and Tobacco Fund' and other good causes, but the general mood was one of grim determination. The local economy, however, did quite well out of the war. Although the chicken fattening business declined steeply as feed costs rose and poultry prices were fixed, producers turned to selling eggs, the price of which soared. More land was put back into production for food. There was also a big demand for pit props to replace supplies from abroad: sometimes as many as 30-40 trucks of them left Heathfield station on a Sunday. The age-old production of charcoal was also given a boost: it was needed for the making of munitions, some of it being used locally for this purpose.[19]

Peacetime brought with it a revival of the chicken fattening industry and a period of moderate prosperity for Heathfield. The new town continued to develop. During the twenties three new banks opened in the High Street, the Plaza cinema was added about 1923 (though with a tin roof which made it difficult to hear during heavy rain storms), as well as a fire station and bus garage. In the thirties the railway station had a staff of twenty-five to cope with the goods and passenger traffic: each Saturday evening a special (and foul-smelling) 'Chicken Express' came into the station with more birds to be fattened.[20]

In the mid thirties the dominance of the new urban complex over the old village was confirmed when it appropriated the name of Heathfield for itself, the original settlement becoming known as 'Old Heathfield'. On this occasion it was the local Chamber of Commerce which took the initiative. Local traders complained that there was considerable confusion because of the existence of 'Heathfield' and 'Heathfield Tower' post offices, and suggested that the latter (in the High Street) should in future be known simply as 'Heathfield' post office, the other being re-named 'Cade Street'.

The matter came before the parish council which in 1935 approved both that change and a suggestion from the Head Postmaster at Eastbourne that the telephone exchange should at the same time drop the name 'Heathfield Tower' in favour of 'Heathfield'. It was also he who decided that the older post office at Cade Street should in future be known as 'Old Heathfield'. But it is doubtful whether he can take the credit (or otherwise) for having invented 'Old Heathfield': he may well have been following – and confirm-

Heathfield High Street in the 1930s

ing – a change in local usage that had already occurred. As for 'Heathfield Tower' that seems to have dropped out of use rather speedily – except for a local branch of the Women's Institute, where it lingered on until the branch itself faded away a few years ago.[21]

It was in the early thirties that the Chamber of Commerce also took the initiative in trying to put an end to the difficulties created by the new town straddling two different parishes. It passed a strong resolution urging an amalgamation of Heathfield and Waldron, together with part of the parish of Hellingly near Horeham Road (later Horam) station. The matter was discussed on 7 April 1932 in a carefully-orchestrated sequence of meetings. First, both parish councils met separately. They then came together for a joint meeting, which was also attended by a representative of the County Council. This voted 15-2 in favour of the proposed merger. Finally, each parish then retired to vote separately, Heathfield voting 11-1 in favour, with one abstention.[22]

Unfortunately, it was not in the power of the parishes themselves to effect the merger. But the following year they did set up a Joint Advisory Committee and in 1934 succeeded in taking common action to resolve a curious problem which had arisen with the Weald Electrical Supply Company.

It appears that the street lights in the two parts of the town were being put out at different times: the two parishes wanted them all kept on until 11pm. The electricity company at first replied that it could not entertain such a suggestion – and that in any case the bulbs in the Waldron part of the town were 75 watts, while those in the Heathfield part were only 60 watts. But it then became clear that it was really a matter of money. The company said it was willing to upgrade the Heathfield street bulbs to 75 watts if the parish council met the additional cost of 2 shillings a lamp, and that if both parishes could agree, it would accept 11 pm for lights out throughout the town. So a little progress was achieved – but it was almost another forty years before a joint council was established in 1973, and only in 1990 that the two parishes were at last able formally to merge.[23]

JAMES GROVES

Life at Heathfield Park itself continued much as before - unlike in many larger country houses and estates. This was a time when a great number of them were experiencing difficulties. There were several reasons for this, including the loss of young male heirs during the wartime slaughter, a significant rise in death-duties in the 1919 budget, and the post-war agricultural depression. Many estates were broken up, and their mansions converted to other uses - like Possingworth Manor which became a hotel in the 1930s.

Heathfield Park was modest enough to survive. It had acquired a new owner in 1919, James Groves, who had ample private means. A Yorkshireman by origin, born in Redcar in 1857, he was a successful shipowner, and the founder of Fargrove Steam Navigation Ltd. Since 1910 he had lived with his wife at Brownings Manor, Framfield, where he had built up a pedigree herd of Sussex cattle and a national reputation as a breeder.[24]

He was sixty-two when he bought Heathfield Park and its estate, which now extended to just over 868 acres. It is not clear why he moved, as he had no immediate heir (his only son having died in 1912) and the change entailed the sale of his prize-winning herd. It may be that he was in search of a more prestigious address: at all events, he and his wife looked the part - he was a tall man, with a white moustache and a monocle, and she a stately-looking woman. He undertook some alterations of the mansion, and maintained both

North Lodge and main entrance to the Park, 1930s

it, and the woodlands of the Park, in very good order. It was during his time that a new plantation was added outside its walls in the triangle of land opposite the Crown hotel. The gardens were also kept in immaculate order, the walled kitchen garden producing a range of exotic fruits including bananas, peaches and nectarines as well as grapes. A future Head Gardener, James Wilson Smith, began working there at this time. Among other members of the extensive staff, several of whom occupied cottages in Portland Square just outside the Park walls, the long-serving gamekeeper, Blacker, is still remembered as a great character, though much feared at the time by local poachers.

Like his predecessors, Groves opened the grounds to the public from time to time, and continued to allow the local cricket club - of which he became president - to play on their accustomed pitch. He also made a gift to the parish council of five acres of land to create the Tower Street recreation ground.[25]

Groves served as a J.P. and was also an active member of the Conservative party. He was president of the Heathfield branch of the Rye division, and one of the founders of the Heathfield and Waldron Constitutional Club. He and his wife took a keen interest in a range of other local activities including the tennis club, the Horticultural Society, and the Nursing Association. They were generous in their support of these and other voluntary bodies, local hospitals and the church. They met the cost of rehanging the existing bells in the parish church in 1921 and added two more as a thanksgiving for the end of the war; contributed to the cost of building St Richards' church hall; and entertained the children of Broad Oak council school each Christmas.

His wife, however, died in December 1924 after only five years at the Park. Groves himself lived on for another eleven, reaching the age of 78. The local paper accounted it a great loss for the district when he died after a short illness in January 1935, leaving an estate valued at £713,570. The funeral and burial service were held at Framfield Parish Church, close to his earlier home in Sussex.

HARRY CLIFFORD-TURNER

The Park and the estate were put up for sale at auction at the White Hart in Lewes on the afternoon of 14 October 1935. It was a sign of the hard times now affecting even modest-sized estates that the two were offered separately. First came the Park itself together with the house, described as a 'most attractive residential property in first rate order' which covered 366 acres. This was followed by the Heathfield Park Estate, extending to 502 acres, which was offered in no less than 53 separate lots. These included Tower Nursery, Satinstown Farm, Little Tottingworth, the Old Half Moon Inn, and numerous houses and cottages close by the Park, among them the estate cottages in Portland Square, and Keeper's Cottage where Blacker had lived. [26]

In the event, the whole of the estate was bought by a single purchaser, Harry Clifford-Turner. He was another self-made man from the City, the founder and senior partner of a well-known and successful firm of solicitors, and for forty years the driving force behind it. He was a big man, physically and otherwise, who had made his way – and become wealthy – by relentless hard work and trust in his own judgment. Not for nothing was he known in his firm as 'The Governor': a term not without affection, but also one which recognised (as his partners also had to recognise) his determination to keep control in his own hands.

Born in Dalston in October 1876, he was one of six children. His father ran a manufacturing and warehouse business, but this collapsed within six months of his birth and his family was plunged into dire straits from which it never fully recovered. Harry left school at fifteen and began working as a clerk to a City solicitor for five shillings a week. But he was clearly determined to rise above this modest beginning: three years later he took out articles with another firm, borrowing the £80 then needed to pay the stamp duty. He always had great

Harry Clifford-Turner

confidence in his abilities and prospects: in 1899 he married in advance of qualifying as a solicitor when he was earning just £3 a week. It was a good decision, the marriage was a happy one stretching over more than forty years.[27]

But at first he had a struggle to make a living. Most of the early clients of the partnership he set up in Finsbury Pavement under the name H.Clifford Turner & Co (the hyphen in his name was added much later in 1925 when he changed it by deed poll) were themselves poor, too. But from about 1905 he moved into the field of company law, and from that point, though seriously troubled by ill-health for the rest of his life, his professional activities flourished: by 1910 he was earning £3000 a year. As he was over-age for military service in the first world war the firm's activities continued to expand, and in the twenties it handled prospectuses for the Daily Mail and other Rothermere newspapers, was involved in a particularly important flotation for Imperial Airways, launched the Charterhouse Investment Trust, and was appointed solicitors to Dunlop – a connection which was to last for over fifty years.

Acquiring additional partners, the firm was known between 1926 and 1934 as Clifford-Turner, Hopton and Lawrence. During this period it continued to expand its range of clients, which now included a number of important department and chain stores, such as John Lewis and Montague Burton, as well as bus and air transport companies. This was profitable work: in 1927 Clifford-Turner's share was more than £30,000. And although income dropped for a while following the 1929 stock market crash, it recovered again and in 1934 the firm – now Clifford-Turner & Co – moved into offices in Old Jewry. It had by then become one of only three City solicitors involved in new issues, which in the coming years included several which extended its involvement in air transport – such as Airports (the company which then controlled Gatwick airport), and Airspeed which numbered among its directors Alan Cobham and Nevil Shute.

Clifford-Turner lived in London throughout these years, but from time to time took his family to the sea at Brighton. It is perhaps through this Sussex connection that he became aware of Heathfield Park, which he bought in October 1935. By then he was 59 years old, and his four sons grown up (his only daughter had died in infancy). So he did not buy it as a family base, but rather as a weekend retreat from his hectic life in the City. Nevertheless, like most owners before and since, he completely overhauled the mansion, replanned it, and fitted it out at lavish expense. Nor was this a place that could simply be locked up and left when no member of the family was there. One of his sons, who used to accompany him when he drove down from town on Friday evenings, recalled that he maintained a dozen indoor staff including a housekeeper, two butlers and two cooks as well as eight gardeners.

On two occasions, in 1936 and 1937, the Park became the venue for the firm's annual outing. These were jolly, if rather patriarchal, affairs. The staff was brought down in the morning by coach from Old Jewry which left at 9am, arriving in time for a stroll around the Park and its gardens before lunch in a marquee erected on the lawn. Afterwards there were various games, tournaments and competitions, 'mostly of a not very serious nature', and after tea, dancing in the marquee to a Roumanian band followed by the distribution of prizes. The returning coach was programmed to depart at twenty past seven precisely.[28]

In 1937 the afternoon entertainment included a ladies' ankle competition judged by Raymond Clifford-Turner, one of the sons of 'The Governor', who later followed his father to become senior partner in the firm. According to his own account he tried, unsuccessfully, to match the neatest ankle with the prettiest face. This was not the first or only occasion on which young women working for the firm got the better of the men in charge. Harry Clifford-Turner always insisted that they should wear stockings as well as dresses with sleeves. One day, having observed a stockingless female and summoned her to his office, he was surprised to find her properly dressed – a rapid change having taken place with a colleague in the meantime.[29]

Clifford-Turner lent the park for a fete in 1936 organised by the local Conservative party, of which he was elected president in February 1940. But he did not otherwise have time enough to become much involved in local affairs. By then, in any case, the country was at war again. The partners had already considered in 1938, at the time of the Munich crisis, whether in the case of war the firm might be run from the Park, but this idea was not pursued. Clifford-Turner, whose health was deteriorating, was advised by his doctor, Lord Horder, to seek tranquillity in a more secure place, and took a house in

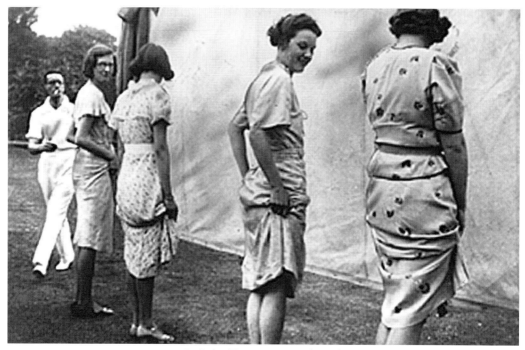

Ladies' ankle competition in the Park

Devon. He remained there until February 1941 – still exercising a good deal of influence over his firm by remote control – when he moved to Inkpen, near Newbury, where he died on 11 June.

WARTIME SALE OF ESTATE

The whole of the Heathfield Park estate of 865 acres was put on the market at an auction sale held at St Richard's church hall on the afternoon of Tuesday 14 April 1942. It was first offered as a whole, and when no offer was made, in 24 separate lots. The smaller properties were all sold: this marked an important moment in the history of the park, for the estate was now reduced to the area within the park walls, a modest 350 acres or so.

But there was no bid for the remaining core of the estate, consisting of the mansion and its surrounding park. This was hardly surprising for it was the middle of the war and – as the sale particulars noted – this part of the estate had been requisitioned (at a rental of £875.2s.6d a year) and was now 'in the occupation of HM Government'. It had also been turned into an armed camp – some of the secrets of which can only now be told.

10. WORLD WAR II: SECRETS OF AN ARMED CAMP (1940–1945)

In September 1939 Sussex was formally designated a 'safe area' and throughout that month evacuees from London and elsewhere poured into the county. But once the period of the 'phoney war' came to an end early the following summer, the county again found itself in the front line, as it had been during the Napoleonic wars and on other occasions in the more distant past. The German invasion plan 'Sealion' drawn up after the defeat of the Allied armies on the continent in the early summer of 1940 targeted the Kent and Sussex coast for the initial assault, with the aim of establishing a beachead running from west of Bognor Regis inland towards Petworth and Ardingly and then east to reach the Kent coast just south of Canterbury. Heathfield was to have been seized as part of this first area of occupation, no doubt because of its strategic position commanding the low-lying ground between the Downs and the edge of the High Weald.

The defence of the Kent and Sussex beaches and their hinterland was the most urgent priority for the new British government, headed by Winston Churchill, which came into office at this critical moment in May 1940. Like most other estates and many large houses in the area, Heathfield Park was

Heathfield Home Guard c. 1943/4

requisitioned by the War Office and turned over to the military authorities. In the wake of the evacuation of the British Expeditionary Force from Dunkirk, they desperately began preparing for the threatened invasion. As coastal defences were hurriedly erected, the conversion of the Park into an armed camp began.

Some of the first to use it were the Local Defence Volunteers, later re-named the Home Guard (and now best remembered as 'Dad's Army'). A number of Heathfield men became officers in the 18th (Crowborough) Battalion, but others were assigned to the 20th (Hailsham) Battalion, with D Company having its headquarters at St Richard's church hall. This did some of its training at a firing range just inside the Park. The Gibraltar Tower close by provided a splendid place of vantage as an observation post with views for miles around. It was there the Home Guard established a nightly vigil, connected by field telephone with the Half Moon pub. They kept themselves warm with a log fire in the upper room of the tower: later on, a similar fire on the ground floor used by regular troops got out of hand and the local fire brigade had to be called out to deal with it.[1]

The house itself was used as a divisional headquarters by a succession of units, both British and Canadian. The 55th (West Lancashire) Infantry Division were among the first regular troops to be stationed there, with their artillery and signals commands being billeted nearby in Heathfield House. The first Canadians arrived to replace them in the summer of 1941: they were to be the main occupants of the Park in the following years. But in the period leading up to D-Day in June 1944 it became the headquarters of the Guards Armoured Division, and also housed a battalion of the Worcesters, as well as some elements of 55 Div which returned for home defence duties.

To try to reconstruct all the comings and goings during these years would be tedious as well as difficult. But what can now be done, for the first time, is to tell the story of some of the more striking of the activities that went on there.

THE 'SECRET SWEETIES'

One of the most extraordinary – and highly secret – of these was located in an unobtrusive hut just inside the Park walls on the left of the entrance from Tower Street. It was there that three young women, junior offi-cers in the ATS (Auxiliary Territorial Service – the curiously neutral title for the all-female branch of the army) manned a communications unit which was part of the British Resistance organisation created in case of German invasion.

Nearby, further into the Park, was a hidden underground hideout from which they were to operate should the location be overrun and occupied.

The organisation to which they belonged consisted of two distinct parts, one for guerilla activities, the other for intelligence work. The first of these was set up during 1940 by Major Colin Gubbins. It consisted of a number of small groups ('patrols') trained to operate from underground hideouts behind the German lines. The first were organised in Kent; by the end of the year there were about 300 of them in various coastal locations. Their members sported Home Guard uniforms, but kept themselves very much to themselves: officially they were known by the bland name of 'Auxiliary Units'.[2]

In November 1940 a second but separate part of the organisation – the 'Special Duties Section'– was created to provide intelligence from behind the German lines in the event of an invasion. Special Duties Intelligence Officers moved into coastal areas to recruit and train the spies who would provide the information. (Some of them are still around: they tell amazing stories about how they were expected to operate in case of need – including galloping on horseback across the countryside to dead-letter delivery points in hollow trees).

A communications system was then devised to collect and pass on this information by wireless. Volunteers for this task were sought from among the ranks of the ATS by its Chief Controller, Lady Carlisle: 43 of them were recruited in the course of 1941. But in November of that year it was decided to expand their number and a special appointment was made for this purpose. The person selected was a senior commander in the ATS, Beatrice Temple, a great-niece of the famous Archbishop Temple of Canterbury, and a future mayor of Lewes.

It was she who devised a rather more formal recruitment process than the method used up to that point. Potential recruits were first interviewed in the genteel surroundings of Harrods lounge – an unlikely place but a milieu with which most of them would be familiar, given the networks used to identify potential candidates. Those selected for further examination were given a set of instructions which must have been devised by an avid reader of John Buchan. They were required to go by train to Marks Tey in Essex, change there on to the Cambridge line, and get off at Haverhill. There they were to cross the road to the Rose and Crown pub where they would be met by an army vehicle with the number '490' on its wing. This transported them to a secret destination where they were given a microphone test. They were then returned to Haverhill.

Those who passed this test had to embark on another cloak-and-dagger journey. They received instructions to report to another unlikely address: the

General Post Office at Highworth in Wiltshire, some six miles north-east of Swindon. There they were scrutinised by the postmistress, Mabel Stranks. If satisfied, she rang for transport (again identified by the number 490) to take the recruits to their final destination: Hannington Hall (owned by the Fry family, the Quakers and chocolate makers). This was just five miles to the west of Coleshill House, where the saboteurs were trained, also in great secrecy.

The young women who emerged from this process acquired a reputation for being exceptionally pretty: they were known as 'the Secret Sweeties'. But the job for which they were trained would have been very dangerous – and probably short-lived – had the Germans ever arrived. In practice, while waiting for this not to happen, it was excruciatingly dull and boring. Miss Temple was once asked 'What exactly do your officers do ? We hear that they sit in caves all day and knit'.

'Secret Sweeties' in training, 1941
Front row: Beatrice Temple, centre; Wynne Read, extreme right

In fact they manned what were known as 'control stations' – or 'zero stations' from the suffix added to to their code name each time they transmitted – and were set up to receive and pass on intelligence from the spy network. There were two of these in Sussex, one at Ardingly, the other in Heathfield Park.

It was to the latter that ATS Subaltern Winifred ('Wynne') Read was posted on the completion of her training in the early autumn of 1941. She had been recruited in the first wave of volunteers in the summer of that year when she was working near Sidcup as a private in the Pay Corps. Once in the 'Auxiliary Units, Signals' she had been trained in wireless telegraphy at Challock Lees, north of Ashford – to the great amusement of the local lads who mimicked the trainees as they heard them practising their call signs 'Hello Lettuce', 'Hello Cucumber' through the open windows of their army huts.

After a brief spell at an Officer Corps Training Unit (OCTU) at Edinburgh, and a one-night visit to the Haverhill centre (where she recalls they had to sleep on bare boards in spite of their new officer status), she was posted to Heathfield – together with two other young ATS officers, Marjorie Barden and Marjorie Filer. All were billeted with families in the vicinity, Wynne Read herself with the Angoods in Tower Street.

The control station in the Park, like those elsewhere, consisted of a hut equipped with wireless receiving and transmitting equipment where the ATS officers worked each day, and a secret underground hideout into which they were to retreat should the Germans arrive. Access to the one in Heathfield Park was gained by pulling back a loose piece of bark on a tree, and pressing the switch concealed under it. The earth about fifty feet away then opened up to reveal a trap door which in turn led to a ladder into a small room. The walls of this room were packed with explosives and ammunition, but under a shelf another catch gave access to a further room equipped with an emergency receiver and transmitter, food, clothing and bunks. Beyond this again was a chemical wc and an emergency escape tunnel.[3]

It is possible that this hideout is still in the Park, though most of them were blown up at the end of the war, and on a subsequent visit Miss Temple was unable to identify its location. Fortunately it never had to be used: instead the trio of ATS officers spent their days manning the wireless equipment in their hut listening in for the daily coded messages sent in, as a matter of routine, by their network of potential spies. These were based on various unlikely texts – including some of the comic verses contributed to *Punch* by Patrick Barrington (later the 11th Viscount Barrington), one of which began :

> 'I had a duck-billed platypus when I was up at Trinity,
> For whom I developed a remarkable affinity.
> He used to live in lodgings with myself and Arthur Purvis,
> And we all went up together for the Diplomatic Service.'

It was equally typically of the operation that the hut was only manned during normal office hours – it seems to have been assumed that the Germans would not be so ungentlemanly as to attempt anything nasty at other times. It was indeed fortunate that, as one of those involved recalls: 'nothing ever happened'.

Nevertheless, the operation was maintained long after any danger of invasion had passed. Perhaps the communications network was then used for other purposes, but it may simply have continued through inertia. At all events, the secrecy that went with it was rigorously maintained. Even the commanding officer of the unit to which the ATS officers were attached was repulsed when he attempted to penetrate into their hut. So too was Police Constable Stanley Newman when he tried to gain access following the suicide by carbon monoxide poisoning on 12 November 1943 of Betty Berkeley, one of the ATS subalterns manning the post – a sad footnote to one of the more exotic activities in the wartime Park.[4]

MONTY AND THE CANADIANS

From the middle of 1941 until late in 1943 by far the largest contingent of troops in Heathfield Park were the Canadians. The first of these to arrive, in June 1941, were headquarters staff of the Canadian 2nd Division. They took over from troops of the British 55th ('Red Rose') Infantry Division, initially while it went to Aldershot for training, and then more permanently in the autumn when Canadian troops became responsible for the defence of the whole of the Sussex coast.[5]

On 17 November that year these troops, together with the rest of the Canadian Corps (totalling some 125,000 officers and men) were detached from GHQ's Reserve and placed, together with the British 12 Corps, under South-Eastern Command. It was on that same day that Lieutenant-General Bernard Montgomery took up his new post as GOC of that Command.

At this stage in the war Montgomery had yet to acquire the high public profile and renown, as well as the military success, which followed his later exploits at El Alamein and the North African desert. But he was a highly professional soldier who had been in the army since 1901. He had seen service on the western front in the first world war (where he was lucky to survive at the battle of Mons), in Ireland during the troubles of the early twenties, and subsequently in Palestine, Egypt and India. Not everyone, however, approved of his brusque manner and idiosyncratic ideas: he had to wait until 1937 before being promoted to Brigadier and given command of the 9th Infantry Brigade back home.

At the outbreak of the second world war Montgomery was in command of the 3rd Division. He crossed to France with them in late September 1939 – and retreated, in good order, with them to Dunkirk the following May. In July 1940 he was promoted to Lieutenant General and took over command of 5th Corps which was responsible for the defence of the south coast from Bognor to Lyme Regis. The following April he was moved sideways (both geographically and otherwise) to the command of 12 Corps in Kent but six months later he was promoted Commander-in-Chief of South-Eastern Command.[6]

Montgomery and the Canadian Prime Minister, Mr McKenzie King, 1941

He came with a formidable, and for some, a terrifying reputation. He was convinced that drastic measures had to be taken if the British army was to be able to deal with the highly professional Germans. Many of those in positions of command were simply incompetent and had to be removed; the whole army had to become far more physically tough and fit; distractions (meaning wives and camp followers) had to be removed; a new offensive strategy had to be developed as well as the capacity to carry it out; and, above all, a new spirit of determination and confidence – what he called 'binge' – had to be nurtured.

Characteristically, one of his first acts was to re-name his command the 'South Eastern Army' and style himself 'Army Commander'. This was part of a calculated policy to give a sense of identity and cohesion to all those under his command. But its immediate impact on the Canadians was to confirm all their worst fears about him. Both of their senior officers in Britain, Lt-General McNaughton and Major-General Crerar, bitterly resented being placed under Montgomery. This was partly a matter of national pride, wishing to maintain an autonomous role for the Canadian troops, and partly a dislike of Monty's brusque personality and style. Well into the Spring of 1942 the Canadians insisted on addressing correspondence to 'South Eastern Command' rather than to 'South Eastern Army'.

It was against this background that Monty set about introducing the reforms he had already imposed elsewhere. He insisted that the Canadians, like the British troops under his command, should adopt a more systematic approach to training, and at the same time change their strategy for the defence of their area – arguing that static linear defences should be replaced by a more mobile defence of crucial localities.

On 28 November he embarked on a visit to the 2nd Canadian Division, and it was probably at this time that he came to Heathfield Park. According to a local eyewitness who was on the civilian staff of the Royal Engineers in the Park at the time, he set up his office in a 30-foot bell-tent pitched on the lawn in front of the mansion. There he received a stream of visitors. He also instituted and took part himself in pre-breakfast runs around the 3½ mile perimeter wall – not at all popular with the officers, who grumbled about being deprived of their morning tea in bed. It is not clear how long he stayed, but it must have been for some time, as he is reported as having rented and lived in a bungalow at the nearby village of Cowbeech during this period. At all events, he was again in Heathfield on 21 December when he addressed the East Sussex Home Guard, later visiting their fieldcraft school at Burwash.[7]

At the end of that month Monty attended the first Canadian exercise 'Beaver' and on 2 January 1942, addressing all the officers of the Canadian Corps about it, did not spare his criticism of their performance. Crerar took great exception to what was said, and in particular to Monty's criticisms of senior Canadian officers in front of their juniors. To calm him down the Commander in Chief of Home Forces, Sir Alan Brooke, had to intervene, inviting Crerar to lunch. Brooke (later to become Lord Alanbrooke) was a firm ally of Montgomery but, not for the first or last time, also had to exercise considerable diplomacy with him too. The Canadians, he wrote, 'are grand soldiers...But they are very touchy and childlike in many ways. You will therefore have to watch your step with them far more than you would with British troops'. Monty, for his part, thought that neither of the senior Canadians was up to the job: he described McNaughton as 'a useless commander',and Crerar as 'unfit to command an army'. Later he and Brooke agreed 'that fighting the Germans was easier than cooperating with and commanding one's own allies'.[8]

It may have been during this period that an incident occurred which showed the initial scant regard for Monty on the part of the Canadian troops as well as their officers. Forced in the course of an exercise to parade in the rain, they gave him a rough reception when he arrived accompanied by Crerar. He was greeted by rude noises and someone shouted 'Hey Monty, for Christ's sake go home, willya ?' Crerar apologised, but Monty remained unruffled, dismissing it as high spirits. He always had a high regard for the fighting qualities of the men themselves – and apparently accepted the story that they were all chewing gum because it was good for their health.[9]

A decision that Monty took that Spring was to have an important impact on the Canadians in Sussex, including those at Heathfield Park. On the morning of 30 April he visited General McNaughton, now Commander in Chief of the 1st Canadian Army, to propose that it should be the Canadians who should provide the bulk of the troops for the projected raid on Dieppe. The proposal was accepted, and subsequently, at the suggestion of General Crerar commanding the 1st Canadian Corps, the troops for the Dieppe operation were provided by the 2nd Canadian Division, which included those stationed in Heathfield Park.[10]

Monty always regarded the Dieppe project as a peripheral affair, and when it was postponed in July he made it clear he was totally against it being reinstated. Nevertheless the decision was taken to undertake the raid in August, in spite of inadequate support from the sea or air. By then, Monty was already in the Middle East, having been given command – at a time of great crisis- of the Eighth Army.

The disastrous outcome of the raid is well-known. The Germans had no difficulty in repulsing the attack and wreaked havoc among the Canadian troops. Of the 5,000 who set out, almost a thousand lost their lives out of a total of 3367 casualties. The remnants of those who had left from the Park did not go back there, but were sent to a camp at Hellingly.

In the meantime, they had been replaced at the Park in May 1942 by the HQ of the 3rd Canadian Division. They in turn were followed in August by the 1st Canadian Division which stayed until Spring 1943 when they were sent off to take part in the invasion of Sicily. The HQ of the 4th Canadian Armoured Division arrived in June 1943: on 9 July they were visited by the Princess Royal. By then the HQ of 55 Division had also returned to the Park: they stayed there until January 1944 when they were moved to Northern Ireland. It was during this period, in October 1943, that a Halifax bomber, running out of fuel after a raid on Frankfurt, crashed in the Park, killing two of its crew members.

But in these middle years of the war it was the Canadian military presence which dominated the area in and around Heathfield – with units in Possingworth Park, Tanners Manor and Cade House, for instance – as well as

FORM 99

XEASTXSUSSEXXCONSTABULARYXX
SUSSEX POLICE FORCE.

From Albert Hibbs, Sergt.15. SUSSEX CONSTAB To The Superintendent of Police,

Heathfield: 9- OCT 1943 L E W E S.

HAILSHAM 7th, October 1943.

re:- Crashed Halifax Bomber at 01-17 hours, on
Tuesday 5th, October 1943, in Heathfield Park,
-------- HEATHFIELD.--------

I beg to report that, at 01-17 hours, on Tuesday 5th, October 1943
heard a loud crash which I presumed to be an aircraft crash, in the
icinity. A few seconds later I received a telephone message from
rs Stevenson of the Old Half Moon Cottage, Heathfield, that a bomber had
r shed in Heathfield Park, Heathfield, just beyond their residence.
Shortly afterwards P.C. Newman also telephoned to this station to
eport the crash.
I at once went to the spot and met the second engine of the M.F.S
f athfield, which I conducted to the scene, the first engine was already
n attendance, when I arrived.
I found the bomber which had crashed in the trees in Heathfield
ark, to be completely wrecked and on fire, also the surrounding trees. The
ire Brigade extinguished the fire, it could then be seen that Sergt. No.
545876 C.HOLDSWORTH was crushed underneath the rear portion of the fuselag
t was quite obvious that he was dead. With the assistance of the M.F.S.
nd members of the public the wreckage was pulled away by means of ropes
nd the body finally rescued.
The body of Ft Lt: No. 116203 L.E. THOMPSON was also found under-
eath a small pile of wreckage, his clothing caught fire which was
xtinguished and this body also rescued. Both bodies were covered over from
he public gaze by means of their parachutes, and at dawn P.C. Newman and
yself conveyed the bodies to Payne's Mortuary, Old Heathfield. Both bodies
ere in a shocking condition.
P.C. Newman returned to his station on the arrival of SC STRANGE
. later reported to me that the facts had been reported to Sub-Control,
.D. Dept, Lewes, and Hailsham Police Station, also that the other six
 ers of the crew, who were alive, having baled out, had been accounted
or.
A.S.S. Watson then arrived on the scene and made arrangements for
.C. Turner to act as a guard. It C.F.L. St George the O.C. of the local
ome Guard was also contacted and a guard was also mounted by them.
At 11-30 a.m. the same morning the wrecked machine was left in
harge of a Lieutenant, N.C.O. and four privates of the Reconnaissance
orps, stationed at Eastbourne.
Receipts attached for the bodies and personal property.

Lewis Hibbs Sergt.15.

Submitted. The receipts have been retained and filed with the copy
of Crashed Aircraft Report, at Divisional ... D. Dept.

he Asst.Chief Constable,   _W Lamberth_   Inspr.
. No.1 District, Lewes.   For Superintendent.

Crashed bomber : police report

in the rest of Sussex. As a Canadian source admits, their troops became saddled with a reputation for worse behaviour than any other overseas group. There were certainly some rough moments at the Half Moon Inn, just outside the Park walls, much frequented by some of the French Canadians. Locals also tell stories which suggest that there may have been some men from the South Saskatchewan Regiment around: they became known (and not only in Heathfield) as 'the Sirloin Steak Rustlers'. Many of the local girls also took care not to go out alone. But on the other hand, quite a number of them, like those elsewhere, married Canadian servicemen.[11]

PREPARING FOR OVERLORD

From the early months of 1944 Sussex became one of the concentration areas for the troops massing for the invasion of the continent and the Park, like the surrounding area, filled up with more and more troops and equipment.

At the end of April it became the headquarters of the Guards Armoured Division, commanded by Major General Sir Allan Adair. Other HQ units were located close by – the Royal Artillery and RASC in Heathfield House, for instance, and REME in Cade House. Security in and around the Park was now very tight, with many armed patrols and guard dogs, and much barbed wire. Certain places and areas were particularly heavily guarded, including the house itself where passes had to be shown to enter. Inside, the servants' staircase was blocked off with rolls of barbed wire, which were also used to protect the attic windows. 'There, in a top-floor room, the building wired in and guarded day and night', Sir Allan recalls, 'was unfolded the plan for D-Day'.[12]

Outside, in the Park, there were also guards around the Nissan huts where captured German and Italian airmen were interrogated before being sent on elsewhere. And, down in the southern recesses of the woods, a large underground bunker was constructed for use in an emergency, designed to be both bomb- and gas- proof.

Clearly important work was going on at the Park, as the Germans themselves appear to have realised too. Their reconnaissance planes frequently flew low over overhead. They did not attempt, however, to attack. It was only later that a flying bomb landed and blew up there, but by then the invasion forces had long since departed.

Another unit which arrived in the Park to take part in Overlord was the 1st Battalion of the Worcesters. Having done their training elsewhere in the county, and been inspected by Monty, they arrived on 15 April 1944. There were about five thousand of them, and they had to live in tents. They occupied themselves with their final preparations - loading trials, waterproofing, rope climbing and swimming in the lakes. But as May arrived there was time for a little cricket, and on 1 June they were given permission to celebrate, on a modest scale, their annual regimental occasion. In the afternoon a fun-fair took place on the cricket ground, with each platoon contributing a side-show. At one stage two generals were seen competing vigorously to 'Wet the Worcestershire Wench', at three shots a penny. It was all a tremendous success, according to the regimental historian.[13]

On D plus seven a small advance party of the Worcesters left, followed three days later by their transport, and on D plus 12 by the foot soldiers. The main party crossed to Normandy on 18 June on the Southern Railways ferry *Canterbury*: they were the first to do so in the wake of the gale which created havoc off the landing beaches. The sea was still very choppy: they had a rough time of it before they were landed three miles east of Arromanches. Nor did things go well on the other side: the infantry failed to meet up for some time with their motorised units, and then suffered heavy casualties in the fierce fighting around Caen. In just over a month the Worcesters lost twenty officers and half of the men in their rifle companies, before they were withdrawn for a rest.

The Guards Armoured Division had a similar experience. It was scheduled to land in Normandy on D plus 18, and an advance party, including the divisional commander, left on 12 June and sailed the following day from George V dock near Tilbury. But that evening they were caught off the Normandy coast by the same gale and were unable to land for five days. In the meantime the rest of the Division had also left - an eyewitness reports that it took two days for the tanks and other equipment in the Park to depart. It was not until the end of the month that the whole of the Division got across to Normandy. Two weeks later it was used in Operation Goodwood, a major attack east of Caen which turned into a prolonged and bloody battle. It was also subsequently involved in heavy fighting in western Normandy before the breakthrough which enabled it make a dash across northern France and into Belgium. The Division liberated Brussels on 3 September.[14]

As the invasion forces moved further towards the heartland of the continent, the habitual calm of the Park began to reassert itself, awaiting the return of peacetime.

11. A CHANGED WORLD: PRIVATE AND PUBLIC INTERESTS (1946-1993)

When peace returned in 1945 it brought many changes in its train – not least for owners of country houses and estates throughout the country.

It was already clear in the closing stages of the war that important social changes were in the offing. The pressure for change was then greatly increased by the election in 1945 of the Labour party under Clement Attlee which swept into power determined to diminish the social disparities of the past and to improve the lot of the generality of the population. Although the measures it took fell far short of the socialist revolution which some had feared, those with large country houses living off inherited wealth felt themselves for a while to be part of a besieged minority, struggling to survive.

Many were faced by the need to undertake large capital investment to restore and refurbish their properties and land neglected or damaged during the war. Not all were able to find the means to do so. In some cases death duties also became a crippling burden. During the ten years between 1945 and 1955 more country houses were deliberately demolished or allowed to decay than at any previous period in the century. Others were off-loaded into public ownership through the National Trust by those unable or unwilling to maintain them any longer. The reduction in the size of estates was also part of the same process. In 1957, for instance, death duties of £400,000 led to the sale of 31 of the 61 farms on the Ashburnham estate.[1]

For both the larger country houses and the smaller ones like Heathfield Park there were also other problems. One of the most important was the shortage of domestic labour. The needs of reconstruction and the availability of alternative employment for women meant that the supply of willing hands, which had for so long ministered to the daily needs of the wealthier members of society, was now much diminished. Domestic service had also become far less desirable and acceptable as a form of employment. So many country houses – including Heathfield Park in the 1950s – had to make do with the remnants of an older generation of servants, supplemented by younger staff recruited from abroad, sometimes from far-flung places. As a consequence of the general labour shortage, the costs of employing experienced staff rose sharply, adding to the financial burden of country house owners – or the inconvenience of life as staff numbers were reduced.

South Wealden Local Plan

Written Statement and Proposals Map

Adopted Plan

Wealden
District Council

Planning Document, 1992

Another set of problems arose from the increasing intervention of public authorities in the freedom of action of private owners through planning legislation.

The 1932 Town and Country Planning Act had already introduced some measures designed to combat urban sprawl and protect the countryside. It was under its provisions that in April 1940 an agreement was reached between Clifford-Turner and Hailsham RDC about the designation of part of the park around its central ghyll as a 'private open space' and restrictions on any residential development in the rest of the park.

The 1947 Town and Country Planning Act went much further. It not only obliged each relevant local authority to draw up a development plan for its area, indicating the uses to which land could be put, but also required owners of land to apply for permission when a change of use was proposed. It also laid down the principle that profiting from development was not a right but a privilege to be exercised at the discretion of public authorities, with part of the profits going to the public purse.

Although this latter provision did not long survive, owners of land had now lost the right to develop it at their own discretion. Planning permission for most types of development was now required, and over the following years further legislation and ministerial decrees steadily tightened the requirements of the planning process. At the same time, increasing concern with the protection of the environment also led to a stream of other measures, of both a statutory and non-statutory nature, designed to safeguard the countryside and its ecology, historic buildings, parks and other open spaces. A whole new bureaucratic apparatus came into being at both national and local level to ensure compliance with these requirements.

However necessary and desirable, all this placed on country house owners significant new restraints and obligations with which they had to comply. They did not always find this easy or agreeable - as the controversies which first arose in the 1970s over developments in Heathfield Park showed all too clearly.

A BLUNT RETURNS

It was some years, however, before the full impact of these changed conditions was felt at the Park. They were in any case masked for a while by the return of a member of the Blunt family into ownership. The old order, it seemed, was being restored.

Following the failure of the attempt to sell the park and its mansion in 1942, the sons of Clifford-Turner who had inherited from their father were anxious to dispose of the property: but it was only in December 1947 that they finally succeeded in doing so. It is possible that Sir John Blunt, 10th Bt., had earlier become a tenant: he remarried in 1947 and the purchase was made in the name of his new wife, Lady Margaret Hunam Blunt. The price was a relatively modest sum in the region of £40,000.[2]

Sir John had succeeded to the title in 1938 on the death of his father who had continued the family's links with Empire, serving with the Imperial Yeomanry during the Boer War (1899-1902) and subsequently as a captain in the Natal Border police. His son, born in 1908, had also followed a military career, in the 10th Hussars, and after the second world war he travelled extensively on government service. His first marriage ended in divorce in 1941. His second wife, described by one acquaintance as 'devastatingly beautiful', was the former wife of the 2nd Viscount Rothermere, and a one-time friend of the Aga Khan. (One of the latter's presents to her, a gold and blue brocade coat, surfaced in the Sotheby's sale at the Park in 1993).[3]

Sir John was a well-built, impressive figure in his late thirties when he resumed the family connection with Heathfield Park. Both he and his new wife shared a passion for breeding and racing horses, and Sir John certainly aspired to play to the full the role of a country gentleman. But he soon acquired a reputation for being, as one local put it, 'a poor nobleman': his resources never quite matched his aspirations. He drank heavily, talked a great deal, and had always a keen eye for the ladies. He was also known locally as something of an eccentric who, for instance, kept chickens in the basement of the mansion, and never came to terms with even simple electrical equipment.

He and his wife did not survive long at the Park: it was sold again in October 1948, and they moved to Cross Farm at Waldron (now a well-known

Park gates, 1950s

local vineyard). Sir John's second marriage also petered out, his wife leaving
him to set up an Arabian stud at Mayfield. He continued to nurture ambitious
projects but also behaved in unpredictable ways: for instance, a decision to
build a library in his new home did not prevent him having a bonfire of family
records and books. He died in 1969 and was buried in the family vault in the
churchyard at Old Heathfield.[4]

THE FITZGERALDS

The succeeding owners, the Fitzgeralds, were much grander, and had a much
greater sense of style. And although they traded down-market in coming
to Heathfield Park from a larger place at Newmarket, there was inherited
Sassoon money to sustain them in comfort and elegance in their new home.

Captain Derek Joseph Barrington Fitzgerald was a handsome, dashing but
relatively impecunious Irishman. He was the only son of the Hon. Eustace

Robert Southwell Fitzgerald, who in turn was the fifth son of Baron Fitzgerald, a Lord of Appeal in Ordinary from 1882 to 1889. He served in the Irish Guards during the first world war. One of his fellow officers was Reginald Sassoon: it was through him that he was introduced to his sister Violet Leah Sassoon. They married in 1917 when they were both in their mid-twenties. Fitzgerald was then caught up in the exciting world created by that extraordinary, talented, and successful family.[5]

The Sassoons had a quite remarkable background. Until the 19th century the family had been, for well over two thousand years, part of a Jewish community living in Baghdad. Originally established there, it is claimed, by Nebuchadnezzer after the capture of Jerusalem they successfully survived over the centuries a succession of rulers including Persians, Greeks, Romans, Parthians, Arabs and Mongols. They retained their identity while dressing like Arabs, eating like them, speaking Arabic and even adopting some of their customs, including - if in a modified form - the harem.

Many of the members of this Jewish community lived perpetually on the verge of starvation, but the family through which the Sassoons trace their ancestry rose to prominence as merchants and financiers. In the late 18th century one of their number, Sassoon ben Saleh, became the Chief Treasurer to the Turkish ruler, Ahmet Pasha. It was one of his sons, born in 1793 and originally known as David ben Sassoon, who became the founder of the modern Sassoon dynasty. Forced to flee in 1829 with his father from Baghdad in the face of an imminent threat of persecution, the family moved to Bombay. It was there he laid the foundations of the astonishing transformation of the family, in a single generation, from their oriental origins to successful and highly sophisticated members of London society.

From his new base in India David Sassoon rapidly developed trade between western India and the middle East, later extending it into central Asia, southern China and Japan, and establishing a virtual monopoly in the importation into India of fabrics, cotton yarn and opium. In due course his firm, David Sassoon and Company, also began to import textiles from Lancashire and, during the American civil war in 1864-6, to export cotton thread there.

In building up this trading empire, David Sassoon made good use of eight sons (he had 14 children in all, from two marriages). But after his death in 1864 there was a rift in their ranks, his second son setting up in 1867 a rival company - Messrs E.D. Sassoon & Co - which competed fiercely, and successfully, with the original family firm. Although the main headquarters of the new company remained in Bombay, a presence was also established in many other trading centres, including London and Manchester. In the 1880s it was from palatial offices in Fenchurch Street that two members of the next generation, Jacob and Meyer Elias Sassoon, directed its activities in Britain. The latter lived in great style with his wife and family in Hamilton Place, at the Hyde Park end of Piccadilly, where they entertained on a grand scale, their balls, dinners and entertainments becoming a feature of Edwardian London. Other members of the family had in the meantime become close friends of Prince Edward himself and prominent members of his Marlborough House set, receiving honours at his hands once he ascended the throne.

It was a daughter of Meyer Elias Sassoon, Violet Leah - a great-grand-daughter of the Baghdad patriarch, David Sassoon - whom Captain Fitzgerald married. She was a member of the fourth generation of the family which, in sharp contrast to its predecessors, failed to produce many male heirs, leading one historian of the family to announce 'the extinction of the House of Sassoon'.[6]

Two male members of that generation nevertheless achieved great distinction. One was her cousin Siegfried Sassoon, the writer, whose searing description of life (and death) in the trenches of the first world war in both poetry and prose brought great acclaim and a permanent place in English literature. The other was Philip (later Sir Philip) Sassoon, MP for Hythe from 1911 until his death in 1939. During the inter-war years he occupied a succession of ministerial offices and played an important role as host to high-level informal political gatherings at his country seat, Port Lympne, on the Romney Marshes. He also became, with his sister, a leading figure in the social and artistic life of the capital at his London home in Park Lane.[7]

It was this world that Derek Fitzgerald entered following his marriage. At the same time it also provided him with a new career in the Sassoon business empire. He became a director of E.D.Sassoon and Company Ltd, of the E.D.Sassoon Banking Company Ltd, of the British Burma Petroleum Company, and of the Eastern Bank. In 1941 he was described as 'the man at the heart of various E.D.Sassoon interests' and 'a considerable figure in the City of London'. The same source added: 'The Sassoon genius has turned to the advantage of the Irishman - and why not ?'[8]

By the time he and his wife arrived at Heathfield Park in 1948 they were in their fifties, and their only son was already married. They used Heathfield Park as their country residence, but continued to maintain a flat in London, and also travelled extensively. There were long periods when they were away and the blinds were drawn. And although they normally spent Christmas at the Park, often on their own, each January they departed to seek the sun, heralding an intensive and early Spring-cleaning by their staff.

There were still some 15 or 16 of these, most of them living in but others occupying houses and cottages in the vicinity. They included a butler, chauffeur, valet, housemaid, under-housemaid, ladies' maid, kitchen maid, cook, three or four gardeners, a herdsman, dairy man, odd-job man and a cleaning lady. The core of the staff were of advancing years, while – as a sign of changing times – some of the younger ones came from far-off places. One of these was recruited in 1952 on a two-year contract by an agency from her native St Helena, being paid a modest £2-10s a week. She later married a local man and, as Millie Avard, settled in the village.

The Fitzgeralds furnished the house with their collection of English and French furniture and adorned the walls with a remarkable array of paintings from a variety of periods, including the French impressionists. Some of these came from the extensive collection made by Mrs Fitzgerald's father: others she acquired herself. When they were auctioned in 1963 they 'excited world markets' and fetched record prices. One of them, *La Belle Strasbourgeoise* by Nicholas de Largillièrre was bought by the City of Strasbourg for £145,000.[9]

View towards the cricket ground

The High Street in the 1950s

Both the house and its gardens were kept in immaculate order, but it was a very private world that the Fitzgeralds created. There was little contact with the local community, other than through occasional gestures such as the provision of flowers for the parish church at Easter and Christmas. They did however entertain on a considerable scale, and regularly during the season at Glyndebourne. Each year the Duke of Norfolk brought a cricket party to play the local team on the ground within the Park walls. The Fitzgeralds were also regular visitors to Ascot during the season.

They were nevertheless often on their own. They dined formally, sitting at opposite ends of the table, and afterwards departed to their separate sitting and bedrooms. By 1963, as their staff problems became more acute, they decided that after 15 years of ownership it was time to leave.

HEATHFIELD IN TRANSITION, 1945-65

The lifestyle of the Fitzgeralds during their period at the Park now seems to belong to a rather distant world. But Heathfield itself during the two decades following the second world war was also in many respects a very different place from the one we know today even if its essential characteristics have remained unchanged.

These characteristics – and the problems arising from them – were clearly identified in a report drawn up by the Sussex Rural Community Council at the end of the war. In this, a striking example of the new concern with planning, Heathfield was singled out as an example of the problems of a town which had grown up as a sprawling new development separated from its old village centre. The report pointed out that 'the contours of the district and the situation of Heathfield Park make the by-passing of the township difficult', and concluded that the only solution lay in a re-alignment of the highway from Cross in Hand to Burwash 'and a determination to achieve a more centralised community worthy of the status and functions of a market town'. But although its analysis was acute and prescient, the solution it suggested lay beyond the reach of the authorities concerned – the consequences of which are all too apparent today.[10]

At the time, however, there were far fewer car-owners, and Heathfield itself still had a railway station. It was a quiet place of some 3000 people characterised by small-scale family-run businesses and shops: typical of the atmosphere at that time was the Park View Stores which advertised 'Orders Respectfully Solicited. Personal Supervision'.[11]

But the agricultural life of the district was changing. The cramming of chickens, for so long one of the staple activities, went out with the advent of caponising tablets in about 1948, and chicken-fattening by about 1960 when broilers took over. The familiar windmills of the district – as many as 197 in the county as a whole at the beginning of the century – were down to only 19 by 1969. And the annual Cuckoo Fair which had been held on 14 April at Cade Street, opposite the new Half Moon Inn (now the Jack Cade) was discontinued just after the end of the war.[12]

The town itself nevertheless began to expand. In 1949 a start was made on an extensive new housing estate at Waldron Thorns, just beyond the railway station, while at the other end of the town, in the same year, work at last began on a new secondary school – then called the County Modern school– on a prominent site at Cade Street just outside the entrance to Heathfield Park. Arguments about it siting had been going on since before the war. Many thought that it would disfigure the landscape – and in 1948 it needed the Fine Arts Commission to give its approval and put an end to arguments in the County Council over its design, and particularly its flat roof.[13]

A little further to the east along Cade Street the Village Institute and Goward Hall – both built on land donated by owners of the Park – had only belatedly been handed back by the military. The first dance to be held there after the war was not until St Valentine's Day 1948 – but then 150 people

Sussex

Midway between Tunbridge Wells and Eastbourne, each 16 miles distant
Lewes 14 miles   London 51 miles   Adjacent to Old Heathfield

ILLUSTRATED PARTICULARS, PLAN and CONDITIONS OF SALE

of

HEATHFIELD PARK

The Elegant William and Mary House
in a walled Park with an impressive landscape setting and superb views

Hall; Six Fine Reception Rooms; Seven Principal Bed and Dressing Rooms with Six Bathrooms;
Four Guest Rooms and Bathroom; Four Staff Rooms and Bathroom; Excellent Domestic Offices

Colonnaded Sun Terrace and Broad Walled Terraces

Main Electricity and Water   Oil-fired Central Heating

Garages for several cars and Stabling

EXCEPTIONALLY BEAUTIFUL GARDENS AND TIMBERED GROUNDS

TWO MODERNISED ENTRANCE LODGES

EXCELLENT STONE-BUILT COTTAGE IN VILLAGE

PAIR OF COTTAGES FOR CONVERSION

Buildings and Delightful Sites for Development
(subject to Planning Consent)

WALLED PARKLAND AND WOODLAND

ABOUT 114 ACRES

THE WHOLE WITH VACANT POSSESSION

For Sale by Auction as a Whole or in Nine Lots (unless sold privately) by

TAYLOR & TESTER *and* E. WATSON & SONS

IN THE SALON ON THE PREMISES
on WEDNESDAY, 23rd OCTOBER, 1963, at 3 p.m.

Solicitors: PEARSONS & DRIVER, Pump Court, King's Square, York. *(Tel.: 25661.)*

Joint Auctioneers: TAYLOR & TESTER, 3 King Street, East Grinstead, Sussex, *(Tel.: 4478.)* and at 12 Gloucester
Place, W.1.
E. WATSON & SONS, Estate Offices, Heathfield, Sussex, *(Tel.: 11 and 211.)* and at Wadhurst
(Tel.: 6).

turned up. This was still a time, before the arrival of television in every home, when people sought entertainment in the town. The early fifties were the heyday of the State Hall in Station Road where a series of very successful Dixieland jazz band dances was organised by Horace Relf, secretary of the local British Legion. The first show on Whit Saturday 1952 was a huge success: 550 people packed the hall. For the next three years similar occasions – known as 'The Dancers' Rendezvous' – were organised about every two months, at which some of the most famous bands of the day performed. These included Freddy Randall and his band, Alex Welsh and his Dixieland All Stars, Mick Mulligan and his jazz band, and Sid Phillips. Late-night buses were organised, and people came from all around the surrounding district.[14]

But by August 1955 the peak of the enthusiasm for the dances had passed and no more were organised, the hall being sold in 1962. The Plaza cinema also shut down in the early sixties.

Then, in 1965, came another change of much greater significance: Dr Beeching struck and the passenger service on the Cuckoo Line was closed down. The last steam-hauled passenger trains from Heathfield station ran on 12 June 1965. It was a hot Sunday, and all of them down to Eastbourne were packed, at a return fare of 6/–. Some goods traffic continued for a little longer, until April 1968, but effectively this was the end of an era. The lifeline that had given birth to the new Heathfield had been severed.[15]

THE MOORES

In the meantime important changes were also afoot at Heathfield Park. Although during their period in residence the Fitzgeralds had kept it intact and in good order, the decisions they took on leaving it were to place its future in jeopardy. Rather than putting it on the market as a single unit, in May 1963 Mrs Fitzgerald sold off the mansion and 100 acres to a property development company. Two years later the western part of the park was also sold to the same company. Many estates were at that time being treated in a similar fashion. In this case it meant that for the first time in its history Heathfield Park was no longer in private but corporate ownership, and that the integrity of the historic park was now threatened.

To head off possible local opposition, the new owners – Broadlands Properties Ltd – promptly donated to the Heathfield Park cricket club the land in the park on which successive previous owners had allowed it to play. The company does not seem, however, to have had a very clear idea of what to do with the Park itself. In October 1963 it put up for auction that part of the estate (including a number of smaller properties) which it then owned. But only two of the nine lots were sold and before the end of the month a raft of planning applications was introduced, proposing the conversion of the mansion into offices or a staff training college, a private hotel, a nursing home, a sanatorium, or use by a religious order. The aim was clearly to try to widen the market for the core area of the estate.[16]

At this stage anything seemed possible. But in the event the company did not pursue any of these projects: in January 1964 it found a private buyer and sold the mansion and its surrounding 100 acres to Dr and Mrs Gerald Moore for £34,250 - somewhat less than the reserve price at auction. The immediate threat to that part of the Park was averted. So, too, for the time being was the carving-up of the remainder of the park within its 19th century walls: over a period of eight years the Moores bought up the various segments into which it had been divided. But the new owners were very different from their predecessors. So too was their style of life, and the use they were to make of the western part of the park away from the house.

'Doctor, dentist, poet, painter, sculptor, writer - to Gerald Moore life is the quest - achievement the Holy Grail'. So reads the publisher's blurb to the autobiography of the early life of this 'versatile, gifted man' *Treading in Treacle*, published in 1983. It is a very good characterisation of the person whose activities were to open a new and controversial chapter in the history of the Park.[17]

Gerald Moore was born in London in 1926, 'into its dusty bankrupt August'. It was his father who had gone bankrupt: he was a dentist who had to leave the Rhondda valley where he was practising as a result of an affair with a married woman, and had then lost everything in a fire in his new surgery in Bristol. Unable to pay his dues, he had been struck off the Dental Register. From having been moderately affluent, the family was plunged into poverty:[18]

> 'We lived in cramped, bug-ridden rooms with predatory landladies waiting like hawks for the weekly rent. Non-payment was dealt with unmercifully, and I recall we moved frequently. Mother often recounts harrowing tales, still ungraced by nostalgia, of tramping the streets until late at night searching for accommodation'.

Although the family fortunes gradually improved, mainly with the help of the piano lessons given by his mother, unpaid bills continued to dog Gerald Moore's early life, and in 1940 he had to leave Eltham College because his father had not paid his school fees. But, having done well in a nativity play,

ROGER PENNINGTON

Dr Gerald Moore and school party

Gerald was sent at the age of thirteen to the Italia Conti school of drama, and from there found his way into films at Elstree. He played juvenile parts in a number of wartime films, including *Love on the Dole* which starred Deborah Kerr and Wendy Hillier, *The Lamp Still Burns* with Rosamund John, and October Man with John Mills. His most important part was in *Medal For The General*, where he 'enjoyed a brief moment of glory as one of the leading characters in a major wartime movie', alongside Godfrey Tearle, John Laurie, Mable Constandurous and Petula Clark. It was at this time that he also came to know Vivien Leigh, then 'at the peak of her fame and beauty'. She was later to turn up at Heathfield Park unannounced one summer's day, for tea and a chat.[19]

For four years Gerry Moore flourished in that world, in spite of occasional misadventures. On one occasion, for instance, he and a friend annoyed Robert Donat. The director told him: 'I don't care if you're Jesus Christ. Mr Donat doesn't want you on his set. Now bugger off, both of you'. But at the age of seventeen his promising career was cut short when it became apparent that, having reached about five foot three, he was not going to grow any taller. Reluctantly Moore decided that he had to seek his fortune elsewhere. When John Mills got to hear of it, he was furious: 'Christ', he said, 'if that's what you intend, what the hell are you doing in my film ?'[20]

It was at this point that Gerald Moore decided to train to be a dental surgeon. He applied himself to catching up on lost school work and succeeded in getting a place at Guy's medical school. (When asked why he wanted a place there, he replied, 'I was born here, Sir, and Keats, the poet I most admire, was also a student here'). By 1949 he had been admitted by the Royal College of Surgeons, and he subsequently became a Licenciate of Apothecaries Hall, Dublin and an M.Sc of the University of Surrey.

With his extraordinary energy and capacity for hard work he then not only built up a flourishing practice in Harley Street but also acquired and ran a number of old peoples' homes. Two of these, in

Mrs Moore and Prince Feisal of Saudi Arabia

Ealing and New Cross, had operating theatres which were converted for use as abortion clinics when these were legalised in the 'sixties.

He also found time to write poetry, and to paint. He was not only very prolific in both words and images, but seriously aiming at professional recognition of his talents in both domains. In the late 50s and early 60s, for instance, he exhibited in a number of London galleries, including the Whitechapel, two in Bond street, and at Heal's short-lived gallery of modern art – where its opening show also included works by the then unknown David Hockney. During this period he also became a friend of Sir Charles Wheeler, the only sculptor to become president of the Royal Academy, and of a number of British-based Australian artists who at the time were establishing their reputations in London. Gerald Moore himself experimented with a number of styles, including what he called 'figurative expressionism' characterised by strong colours, powerful images, thick impasto paintwork and vigorous brushwork.

It was against this background of artistic achievement and ambitions, as well as a flourishing – and remunerative – professional career that Gerald Moore, having arrived in his late thirties, began to look around for a place in the country. He was also by now a family man, married to the former actress Irene Dyer, and having four children. In the course of looking around for a house reasonably close to London, he and his wife chanced on Heathfield Park, liked it immediately, and bought it from the developers.

In looking back thirty years later on their decision, Dr Moore explained:[21]

> 'I do not come from the ranks of landed gentry and have always faced the risk of being dismissed by rational thinkers as a case of "folie de grandeur"…I have always argued that where one puts down one's roots is not a case of "folie" but self-definition. My late ex-wife and I come from old (hardly humdrum) bourgeoise families – we are proud of this. And we were not unused to filling-out large, elegant domestic spaces.
>
> Irene wanted rural tranquility, good stabling and rides for her horses, I wanted to own and live in a work of art. In the event I was enjoying professional success and it was agreed that the family was prepared to sacrifice fleeting pleasures and leisure opportunities to the more significant existence as torchbearers in the colourful, endless domestic cavalcade of a truly great English country house.'

Dr Moore continued his London activities, for a while driving up and down each day, while they took stock of their new domain. It was magnificent

- but it was also expensive to run. There was only a slim base on which to maintain the 'domestic cavalcade': the staff amounted to no more than two gardeners, whom Moore tried unsuccessfully to persuade to take on other duties, and two au pair girls, who were later replaced by a Spanish couple ('who wrecked two of my cars') and young women brought in from the Phillipines.

Eventually the Moores came to the conclusion, like many other owners of country houses at the time, that they needed to supplement their resources to cope with the running costs. Already in 1965 they obtained permission to use the indoor riding school for commercial as well as private purposes. But more ambitious plans were also considered, perhaps in part as a result of Dr Moore's decision to sell the lucrative abortion clinics after a brush with the General Medical Council over publicity he was alleged to have given to them in a press interview – which at that time was contrary to the rules of the profession.[22]

At all events, in July 1970 a planning application was submitted to Hailsham Rural District Council for the erection of buildings in connection with the proposed use of 250 acres on the western side of the park as botanical and zoological gardens. For the first time in its history part of the park was to be open on a regular basis to the public. It would have to pay for the privilege, but as Dr Moore explained, 'We are not out to make a fortune. Our aim is to raise enough income to make it possible to maintain the house and park in a proper condition. It would be a tragedy if they were allowed to fall into decay'.

The idea of a zoo as an additional attraction for visitors was much in vogue at the time, but it was not one which went down well either with local residents, many of whom voiced their opposition to the project at a public meeting and signed a petition against it, or Hailsham Rural District Council, which rejected it in February 1971. 'People don't want crocodiles, timber wolves and the rest of it. They would prefer to see the park laid out purely as a botanical garden with nature trails and perhaps some deer and wildfowl' said its chairman, Mr C.L.Bergne-Coupland.[23]

So in July that year a new project was submitted proposing a picnic area and nature trails, together with a museum, on 195 acres of the park. In February 1972 the County Council produced, for the first time, an informal District Plan for Heathfield which suggested that the Park had the potential for 'informal recreation', and in September that year the new plan was approved, subject to 14 conditions.

THE WILDLIFE PARK

The park was opened to the public for the first time at Easter 1973. The 'Heathfield Wildlife Park & Gibraltar Tower Gardens' offered a variety of attractions. The Tower had been restored and converted into a museum to commemorate General Eliott, with a paved area outside leading to a bridge over a pool for sealions, and close by a picnic area with a marquee offering refreshments, a display of vintage motor cars, a wartime 'Matilda' tank, and two of Dr Moore's bronze sculptures. A new roadway some one and half miles long had been built linking this area with the bottom lake. Along this a 'fun train' ran, passing on its way some animal enclosures containing deer, Jacob's sheep, llamas, porcupine and zebras and a 'Bird City' where exotic birds were displayed.

The initial reactions of the public were rather mixed. Many were delighted to have the opportunity to visit the park and brought their families to enjoy it. But others were less than enthusiastic. Dr Moore was bombarded with complaints from visitors who said they were not getting value for money. So he decided that he had to expand the facilities on offer. A large Nissan-type hut was erected to provide a permanent shelter for the vintage

Steam rally in the 1970s

ROGER PENNINGTON

cars, and a cafeteria; an antique carousel was brought in and functioned as a childrens' roundabout; a wider variety of animals was introduced - including two elephants, two giraffes, a bison, kangaroos, chimpanzees, and some penguins; and a former Royal Box was brought from Sandown racecourse and erected at the side of the bottom lake. In the course of time various other, rather miscellaneous, attractions were added including two 18ft bronze sculptures by Sir Charles Wheeler - 'Power' and 'Speed'. These had originally been displayed over the entrance to the offices of English Electric in the Aldwych, but had been removed when an American bank took over and pronounced them 'too masculine'. They had then been taken into care by the Greater London Council which loaned them to Dr Moore.[24]

The decision to expand the facilities of the park certainly made it more attractive to the public, and a number of special events were also organised, including a ceremony at which the freedom of the Park was presented to representatives of Gibraltar in memory of General Eliott's defence of the Rock. An annual Steam and Petrol Rally was also held in the Park Meadows, followed on one occasion by a jazz concert given by Acker Bilk and his band. These proved very popular occasions, and the Wildlife Park itself also attracted visitors from far and wide: in 1977 it was claimed that there were 150,000 of them each year, and that the Park had become the top leisure attraction in East Sussex.[25]

By now some local residents were complaining about the traffic generated by the Wildlife Park, and the numbers of cars being parked at weekends on the roads close by. There were also other problems. The decision to expand the range of attractions had involved a much higher level of capital investment than the Moores had initially anticipated – and money was always tight. Evidence began to accumulate that some of the enclosures were not properly secure. Fifteen kangaroos broke out on one occasion in 1973, and a steady stream of other animals followed – including camels, zebras, a porcupine and a sealion. Local protests multiplied.[26]

In the meantime, the Moores had also fallen foul of planning regulations. While some additional items like the installation of the Royal Box had been at least conditionally authorised, other developments had taken place without permission. The problem of regularising the situation was complicated by the reorganisation of local government in 1974. The planning powers previously exercised by Hailsham RDC were transferred to a completely new body, Wealden District Council. It took some time for it to make up its mind what to do.

Eventually, having decided that the Park should not be developed into 'an intensively-used recreation resource' Wealden Council grasped the nettle, and on 30 January 1976 refused most of the outstanding planning applications relating to the Wildlife Park. At the end of July the same year this was followed by 47 Enforcement Notices designed to close it down.[27]

The Moores appealed against this decision, and a Public Inquiry was held in September 1977 at the Goward Hall in Cade Street covering both this and Wealden's subsequent refusal of other applications for plans related to the Wildlife Park. This attracted national as well as local interest, the *News of the World* carrying a critical account of the conditions in which the animals were being kept.[28]

After the usual long interval the Secretary of State pronounced on 29 June 1978. It was a judgement of Solomon: conditional approval was given for the Wildlife zoo, but 27 of the Enforcement Notices were upheld and a year allowed for the removal of unauthorised structures.

At first this was seen by some as a victory for Dr Moore. 'Shock waves as animal park gets the kiss-of-life' proclaimed the Brighton Evening Argus on 4 July. But in fact it was a Pyrrhic victory, and the Moores soon decided to turn in a different direction. The Wildlife Park kept going for one more season, but was then shut down at the end of September 1979, its stock-in-trade being auctioned off in April the following year.[29]

THE EXPANSION OF HEATHFIELD

The end of this first ill-fated venture in the western part of Heathfield Park was certainly not the end of the affair but rather the beginning of a succession of attempts to develop that part of the Park. These did not take place in isolation: they were part of a much wider picture of developments in and around Heathfield during the seventies and eighties. In time, some of these were to have an important impact on attitudes and policies towards the future of the Park itself.

In spite of the closing down of the Cuckoo Line this proved to be a period of expansion for the town, as for the south-east as a whole. Between 1965 and 1971 the population of Heathfield grew at about 6% per annum, a higher rate than other places in the county, to reach 4,000 with a further 1,500 in the surrounding area. The 1972 draft District Plan then encouraged further growth, in line with the general projections for the region, making provision for just over a thousand new houses, concentrated on the southern side of the town.

It was on the basis of these proposals that the developers moved in and began to put forward plans for substantial new housing estates. The largest was for the Green Lane site adjacent to the western boundary of Heathfield Park where Faircloughs sought to build an estate of 389 houses. Wealden Council was not in a strong position when it turned down the proposal, having granted outline planning permission for a similar project in 1975. In spite of a vigorous campaign by many local residents who also opposed the development, the Secretary of State ruled in favour of it following a public inquiry held on 23 April-10 May 1985. Salt was rubbed into the wounds as far as the local protesters were concerned as subsequently the estate continued to expand.

As the town grew, its centre also changed quite dramatically. A small industrial estate was built on the former station yard; another on a green field site in Ghyll road. The old Station Hotel was sold in July 1983, destroyed by fire as it was being pulled down, and then replaced by a Budgens supermarket. Several of the older family businesses, including the local fishmonger, disappeared: most of the local estate agents were bought up by national chains, and the High Street filled up with the offices of building societies. A number of more exotic fast food outlets were also added to the traditional fish and chips.

By the end of the eighties there had been an increase of almost 50% in the housing stock in Heathfield, and its population had climbed to around 6500. As the town expanded, and more and more green fields and woods disappeared, it pressed harder up against the walls of Heathfield Park - and it was not long before developers sought to breach this line of defence.

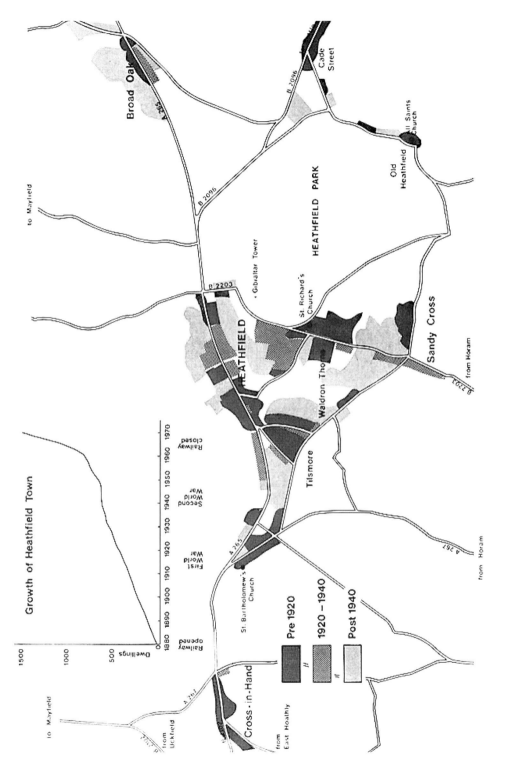

Map and graph showing growth of Heathfield (District Plan, 1972)

THE PARK IN THE EIGHTIES: THE PLANNING FRAMEWORK

As the threat of development in the western part of the Park grew during the eighties, so too did the efforts of national and local authorities to preserve both its historic buildings and the character of the park itself.

Already in October 1952 the house had been included in the Department of the Environment's List of buildings of special architectural interest as Grade Two★. In August 1966 the same status was given to the Gibraltar Tower. This meant that any proposed changes in either would be scrutinised with special care, and be required to safeguard their historical appearance and integrity.

Attention then turned to the protection of the environment and ecology of the park.

Old Heathfield: part of the Conservation Area

ROGER PENNINGTON

In 1979 Old Heathfield, on the eastern side of the Park, was designated a Conservation Area by Wealden District Council, and in October 1983 the whole of the village as well as Heathfield Park were included in the extensive High Weald Area of Outstanding Natural Beauty (AONB in the jargon) designated by the Countryside Commission.

In May 1986 the Nature Conservancy Council (subsequently renamed English Nature) included 101 acres in the eastern half of the Park in its list of Sites of Special Scientific Interest (SSSI) in order to protect the ancient Wealden Ghyll which is notable for its lichen flora. In October the following year the whole of the park was included by English Heritage in its *Register of Gardens and other land of special historical interest*, and in 1989 the Nature Conservancy Council designated part of the western half of the Park as 'ancient semi-natural woodland'.[30]

At the same time the whole process of development control was tightened with further work on the East Sussex County Structure Plan, a revised and updated version of which was published in February 1988, and by the publication in July 1989 by Wealden District Council of the 'deposit' stage version of the Local Plan for South Wealden, including Heathfield.

The policies set out in both these documents showed a much greater concern than in the past with environmental and ecological issues, and with the need to preserve the countryside, particularly those stretches of it which had been singled out as having special merit, from inappropriate or intrusive development. The Local Plan also contained much more detailed prescriptions on certain issues - including Heathfield Park. This now merited a specific policy (15F), which stated:

> 'Land at Heathfield Park, as defined on the Proposals Map, is allocated for leisure/tourism use. Any proposals for development will need to demonstrate the manner in which the environmental and ecological qualities of the Park have been recognised and respected'.

THE PARK UNDER THREAT (1979-93)

The implications of this policy statement were to become a matter of prolonged conflict between the planning authorities and a succession of developers in the years following the closure of the Wildlife Park.

That experience convinced the Moores that it would be better to hand over the task of dealing with the western part of the park to professional developers, rather than to continue to attempt it themselves. By February 1979 it had been leased out to Viking Hotels Ltd which submitted a full planning application for the creation of a leisure centre and nine-hole golf course there. This was to include 100 holiday chalets, and communal buildings including a restaurant, bar, covered pool, squash and tennis courts, a shop, a lounge and games room, and a caravan park.

A complex negotiation then ensued between Wealden Council, Viking Hotels and the owners of the Park. The resulting deal, reached before the summer recess, provided that no proceedings were to be instituted against the Moores for their planning infringements, but while existing authorisations related to the Wildlife Park were to be revoked, Wealden Council was to give conditional approval for the new Leisure Centre and golf course proposal.[31]

At this point it looked as though the new project would go ahead. But then Viking Hotels got cold feet and were replaced by Peacehaven-based developers, Eric, Ian and Paul Hatley, and their company Heathfield Leisure Park Ltd. Having done their sums, they came to the conclusion that the rustic-style log cabins which had originally been proposed would not be good enough for the time-share business which was now their aim. In March 1981 they put in a revised application for a much bigger project, equipped with chalets built of brick, flint and tiles, each with its own cooking facilities.

Suspicions were now aroused that the chalets might become permanent rather than holiday homes, and that a housing estate was in the offing. Permission for this scheme was refused, and Wealden's decision was upheld on appeal by a subsequent public inquiry held in April 1982.[32]

This meant that the developers were left with permission for a scheme that they no longer considered viable or wished to pursue. Not surprisingly, in spite of occasional statements that work was about to begin, nothing happened. In September 1985 the five-year time limit on the permission expired: it was eventually renewed in December 1986 for a further five years. But once again, no action followed.[33]

In the meantime, the Moores had split up, with Mrs Moore remaining in possession of the house and the park. In September 1987 she sold the western half for £70,000 to another Hatley company, Heathfield Leisure Park Developments Ltd. She was also to receive £1500 for each housing plot on that land should planning permission be subsequently obtained. The developers had now decided that a housing project was the thing to go for.[34]

The realisation of their plans, however, was delayed when Nature intervened with the great storm of the night of 15-16 October 1987. The trees in the park took the full force of ferocious winds which gusted up to 100 mph. They wreaked enormous damage: over a thousand mature trees were uprooted, destroyed or severely damaged. The devastation was immense. The roads around the park were blocked by enormous tree trunks which had crashed down on the perimeter wall, destroying long stretches of it. Inside the walls, it was difficult and dangerous to penetrate into parts of the woodland which had been reduced to a nightmare scene of havoc. Huge uprooted trees lay in a tangled mass surrounded by others which had been bent, snapped or stripped of most of their branches. Only the house escaped with minor damage.

Further extensive damage was done in the Park by a second storm which swept through the area on Thursday 25 January 1990: this was less violent, but it brought more trees down and reduced more stretches of the wall to rubble.[35]

The developers did not reveal their hand until December that year when they announced that they were going to apply for planning permission for a new scheme designed by the London-based architects and designers, Dunthorne Parker. This would consist of a public park of 25 acres with various sports facilities; a nature reserve of some 110 acres – and a 'high quality, low density residential park consisting of 149 individual residences set in 47 acres of woodland, a country club with bar, restaurant, swimming pool and other facilities in three acres of grounds'.[36]

Hurricane damage 1987

This time the developers took steps to try to get the local public on their side: they held two open days in the park on 15-16 February and were on hand to explain the advantages of their proposals. Some initial reactions were favourable, but soon attention focussed on the housing estate part of the proposals, and opposition rapidly mobilised. A group of residents living around the park called a meeting in the Goward Hall on the evening of 1 March to express their concern. The support they received led to the creation of the Friends of Heathfield Park, under the chairmanship of Hugh Wylam, to fight the proposals. Later that month at a public meeting called by the parish council and attended by around 300 people, there was almost unanimous opposition to the developers' proposals, and subsequently more than a thousand signatures of protest were collected in the town by the Friends.

The main arguments put forward against the scheme were that it breached the local plan by proposing a residential estate outside the prescribed housing framework for the area; that it could lead to much of the park being covered with houses; that it would in any case threaten the ecology of the rest of the park; that the district was already having difficulty in providing the services to cope with the recent large additions to its population - and that it was altogether too high a price to pay for public access to part of Heathfield Park.

In the face of this public outcry, which was backed by the parish council, Wealden District turned down the proposals in August 1991. The developers then decided that their best course of action was to try to press on with the golf course and leisure centre project - although they had comprehensively rubbished this when arguing the superior merits of the housing estate. They also now faced several additional difficulties. The five-year time-limit on the planning approval which had been renewed in 1986 was due to run out at midnight on 11 December 1991, and they had done nothing in the meantime to meet the conditions the Council had laid down. In August 1991 Wealden Council refused an application to renew the existing planning permission on the grounds, inter alia, that there had been material changes in planning circumstances since the permission had been granted.[37]

The developers then decided to follow a belt-and-braces strategy. They appealed against this refusal to renew the existing permission, and at the same

INDEPENDENT/GLYNN GRIFFITHS

On the eve of the sale, 1993

time belatedly sought to fulfil the conditions attached to that permission. Proposals with this aim were submitted in November, while at the same time some preliminary work was undertaken on the site. But Wealden Council said that they had not been given enough time to consider the proposals before the time-limit expired, and also contested whether a valid start on the works had been made.

In due course both the substance of Wealden's case and their handling of the matter were put to the test at public inquiries. Well before the first of these was held in July 1992 the Secretary of State for the Environment (then Michael Heseltine) decreed that the matter was 'of major significance having more than local significance' and that he would take the final decision on it himself. The outcome, announced in February 1993, was that Wealden was right to have refused a renewal of planning permission. There had been 'substantial changes in planning circumstances' which meant that the project, which it was judged would have 'a very serious harmful effect' on this part of the High Weald AONB, and on the historic park, was no longer acceptable.[38]

By the time of the second public inquiry which was held in September 1993 the company that had launched the appeal had gone bankrupt, and was in the hands of the receivers. And while the recession thus removed one of the protagonists from the scene, natural causes had earlier been responsible for the removal of another.

THE MOORES DEPART

Irene Moore died on 31 May 1992 in sad conditions, having become more and more a recluse. The following March the house and 167 acres of the park were put up for sale at an asking price in the region of £850,000. It was not long on the market, and on Wednesday 19 May 1993 a sale of the contents was held at the park by Sotheby's on behalf of Dr Gerald Moore.[39]

His reappearance attracted a good deal of media attention for what he dubbed 'this brief glimpse into thirty years of the Moore's idiosyncratic dynasty'. Coverage included a BBC2 programme entitled 'Gerry and the Pricemakers'. While most of this concentrated on the preparation and conduct of the sale, it also showed Dr Moore in ebullient form, if a little preoccupied with the prospects for the sale of a considerable number of his own paintings which were also included in it. In the event several of these were sold and Dr Moore was also given a promise of an exhibition in Germany by an admiring dealer. So his farewell to the Park, and return to the west country where he now lives, was not without its compensations.[40]

12. THE PARK TODAY: A FAMILY HOME AGAIN

There was a time, about a thousand years ago, when the Norsemen who arrived in Sussex were bent on plunder, pillage and rape. They were not well received. Fortunately their habits have long since changed, and their presence today occasions little surprise or comment. They are part of an expanding international element in the population which is a direct result of the increasing mobility and interdependence of our world. This is now beginning to be reflected also in the ownership of some country houses – including Heathfield Park, which since 1993 has been owned by the Norwegian family of Inger and Andreas Ove Ugland.

He comes from a family based in Grimstad, a small town on the south coast of Norway, which can trace its ancestors back to the eleventh century. For the last six generations they have been in shipping. Their first boat *The Fortuna*, bought in 1772, plied between southern Norway and England carrying timber in winter and ice in summer. Today the Ugland Group and its associated companies in Norway have interests in 70 ships ranging from car carriers to oil tankers, own a shipyard employing 400 people, and have extensive offshore operations.

Andreas O. Ugland, who was born in March 1955, is the second of three brothers. They spent what he describes as a magical early childhood skiing, climbing and boating before going to the local school in Grimstad. This was quite a different experience from the social segregation of the English public school, and helps to explain the ease and informality of his manner. At an early age he also acquired a taste for dangerous outdoor pursuits and, while absorbing knowledge about shipping in the family circle, demonstrated an interest and flair for business, selling to his brothers and their friends.

These were already the signs of a thrusting, independent personality, and at the age of 15 he sought wider horizons, persuading his parents to send him to boarding school in Switzerland. 'I got on my motor bike and just went', he recalls.[1]

Two years later, in 1975, he followed in the footsteps of several other members of the family and went to study at Newcastle. But whereas they had gone into naval architecture at the University, he went to the Polytechnic (now the University of Northumbria at Newcastle) to take a Higher National Diploma in business and economics. By this time he had teamed up with Inger who was studying art at the same time as pursuing a fashion modelling career in Europe and the United States, at times going back and forth from the US to Paris twice a week. Together they then went to the States, where Andreas acquired BA and MBA degrees at New York University, and Inger a BA in fine arts and interior design (to which she later added a degree in architecture in London).

During a period of work experience Andreas was a manager at Newburg airport in upstate New York when he had to organise the arrival of a group of US hostages freed from Iran. President Carter came to thank him, and present him with a plaque to commemorate the occasion. But shipping was the world he knew, and he set up a ship supply company together with friends in Brooklyn. The experience encouraged him to return to Europe and make his base in London, establishing in 1980 together with his older brother Johan B.Ugland their own ship management company - Ugland Brothers - separate from the Norwegian company, but working closely with it.

Today, sixteen years later, a skilful and enterprising strategy of expansion has made the UK-based operation a sizeable player in its own right, with a number of specialised companies grouped around Ugland International plc, which became a public company following a successful reverse takeover of Bristol Channel Ship Repairers in 1992. The group owns 19 vessels, and manages another 18, mainly container and refrigerated ships.

The urge to succeed and a willingness to take risks are also apparent in Andreas Ugland's favourite sport, power-boat racing. He began at an early age

Inger Ugland

Andreas Ove Ugland

in the Norwegian fjords, building (with his grandfather's help) his first speed-
boat which he drove when he was eight. He had to wait until he was sixteen
to take part in officially-sponsored circuit racing, but then quickly made his
mark, winning competitions and breaking the Nordic speed record for one
class of powerboat.

After returning from the US, he became a serious and successful competi-
tor in offshore powerboat racing, a dangerous high-speed sport which
demands not only considerable financial resources but also great skill and split-
second timing. Together with his team companion Jann Hillestad he won
world championships in Classes III and II, for smaller boats, and then in 1991
entered the select world of the very powerful, high-tech, sponsored racing of
Class I, in which they became European champions in 1993. In the same year
the Ugland team also competed in the prestigious Grand Prix season for a
newly-established world championship, achieving a very creditable sixth place
as well as establishing a new World Speed Record for Class I boats at
144.16mph.

Since then other commitments, both family and work - as well as the
concerns voiced by shareholders about the risks their chairman is taking - have

reduced the amount of time Andreas has been able to devote to the sport. Even so, in 1994 he was awarded the British International Harmsworth Trophy, the oldest and most prestigious trophy in the offshore racing world, for winning all four races in the Martini Endurance series that summer.[2]

THE HOUSE RESTORED, THE PARK REUNITED

The family was living in Hampstead when they saw, immediately liked, and bought Heathfield Park in the Spring of 1993. But a great deal had to be done before they could begin to live in it. The restoration, refurbishment and modernisation of the house, from roof to basement, was a major undertaking. Inger used her knowledge and experience as an architect and interior designer to preserve and enhance the historic features of the mansion while making it into a comfortable, welcoming family house again. The reception rooms on the ground floor, which have always been one of its most attractive features – spacious (but not huge), elegant and light – are once more resplendent. Elsewhere, a more informal atmosphere prevails, especially in the rooms used

Andreas, Nicholay and Alexandra

by the Ugland's three young children - Andreas, Alexandra and Nicholay.

Much work has also been undertaken to restore the grounds and paths around the house, as well as the outbuildings - including the riding stables originally built for the second Lord Heathfield, which now houses a collection of vintage cars. In the park itself deer have been reintroduced, as well as farm animals; tracts of the woodland overgrown with *rhododendron ponticum* have been cleared; and neglected ponds restored.

In the meantime, the fate of the western part of the park, which remained in separate ownership, hung in the balance between 1993 and 1996. In December 1993 Wealden Council applied to the High Court for a decision that the 1986 planning permission for a Leisure Centre was no longer in force, but the Court deferred a decision until the Secretary of State for the Environment had ruled on the appeal by the developers heard at a Public Inquiry held during the autumn of 1993. His decision, in March 1995, to dismiss the appeal lifted a threat of development which had hung over that part of the park for almost twenty years. In the autumn of 1995 it was put on the market by the receivers, and purchased by Andreas and Inger Ugland - thus at last restoring into private ownership the whole of the Park within its 19th century walls.[3]

It is remarkable that Heathfield Park has survived intact - if not wholly unscathed - the various attempted assaults made on it in recent years. This has only been achieved through the vigilance of local authorities and the active support of the Friends and the people of Heathfield. It is to be hoped that private and public interests, having for so long been in opposition over the Park, can now work together for everyone's benefit.

NOTES

ABBREVIATIONS

Courier	*Kent and Sussex Courier.*
DNB	*Dictionary of National Biography.*
ESRO	East Sussex Record Office.
Lucas	Perceval Lucas, *Heathfield Memorials* (1910)
SAC	*Sussex Archaeological Collections*, published by the Sussex Archaeological Society, Lewes.
SNQ	*Sussex Notes and Queries*, published by the Sussex Archaeological Society.
SRS	Sussex Record Society.
VCH	*Victoria County History: Sussex.*

Chapter 2. THE SETTING

1. E. Straker, 'A Wealden Ridgeway', *Sussex Notes and Queries,* vol vi (1936-7) 171-3.

2. Peter Brandon, *The Sussex landscape,* (1974) 55-57; I.D.Margary, *Roman ways in the Weald,* (1948) 262-3; VCH vol I, 478; Martin G.Welch, *Early Anglo-Saxon Sussex,* (1983) Appendix II; Bernard Worssam 'The geology of Wealden iron' in H. Cleere and D.Crossley, *The iron industry of the Weald,* (1985) 53-85.

3. Brandon, op.cit.75

4. D Hazelgrove in Martin Bell, *Excavations at Bishopstone*, SAC vol 115,247 and in Peter Brandon (ed), *The South Saxons,* (1978) 190-202; Martin Welch, *op.cit.* 274-80; VCH vol. IX, 201.

5. A.Mawer and F.M.Stenton, *Place names of Sussex*, Pt II, 463-44, Peter Brandon, (1978) 147 & 152. There are many alternative spellings of Heathfield, including Hadfield (12thc), Hethefeld, Heffeud (13thc) and Heffeld (14thc). VCH, vol X, 200. Later versions included Hethfelde (Saxton 1575), Heathfylde (Norden 1595) and Heathfeild (Speed,1611-12). In the middle of the 19th century it was still being referred to locally as 'Hefful', M.A.Lower, 'Old speech and old manners in Sussex', SAC, xiii (1861) 211.

For Slaughter Common, Lucas 5.

6. D. Hazelgrove in Brandon (1978) 193 & 198-200; VCH, vol IX, 463 n.2.

7. D. Hazelgrove in Martin Bell, *op.cit.*247.

8. W.D. Peckham (ed), 'Thirteen costumals of the Sussex manors of the bishops of Chichester and other documents', SRS 31 (1925) 87-98.

9. Lucas 34-5 claims that there were two fairs from the beginning; VCH vol IX, 201 only one, in June. For 17th century evidence, ESRO ASH 931 and 1178. For the Cuckoo legend, Rev W.D. Parish, *A dictionary of the Sussex dialect and collection of provincialisms in use in the county of Sussex* (1875). New expanded edition by Helena Hall (1957) 28; F.E.Sawyer, 'Sussex folklore and customs connected with the seasons', SAC vol xxxiii (1883) 243-4; Alec Parks, *The old woman of Heffle Cuckoo Fair. Legend and substance* (1987)

10. See maps by Saxton 1575 'Catstret', Norden 1595 'Catestrete, Speed 1611-12 'Catestreet', and Weller 1785.

11. Mawer and Stenton, *op.cit.,* 468 refer to a John Bayle mentioned in a Court Roll for 1391, but the name had been attached to the land at least a century earlier.

Chapter 3. THE HERSTMONCEUX CONNECTION

1. ESRO. Herstmonceux Manor, Calendar of Court Rolls. I owe the reference to this important source to Christopher Whittick.

2. Having failed to answer the court's summons in August 1330 John de Assbourne appeared at its session on 30 October to 'put himself in mercy for many defaults' - only to be hauled before it yet again the following month.

3. Lucas 44. W.D. Cooper's reference in his article 'Participation of Sussex in Cade's rising 1450' in SAC, vol xviii (1866) 18 to 'Sir Thomas Dacre of Baily' has been the source of much confusion: there is no evidence that he owned or lived at Bayley. See I.M.W. Harvey, *Jack Cade's Rebellion of 1450*, (1991) 79 n.34.

4. The survey recording de Monceux's holding also expands on his status as a free tenant. SRS LX (1961) 2. Three successive Johns headed the Monceux family from the late 13th century: this reference must be to the first of them, who died in 1302/3. See also (Rev) Edmund Venables, *The castle of Herstmonceux and its lords* (1851) 15.

5. Venables, *op.cit*.8-14

6. (Sir) Thomas Barrett-Lennard, *An account of the families of Lennard and Barrett* (1908) 154-162

7. ESRO. Manor of Herstmonceux. Transcript of a rental and partial custumal c.1340.

8. ESRO Manor of Herstmonceux, Court Rolls 7 March 1379 and 29 March 1380.

9. Peter Brandon and Brian Short, *The South East from AD 1000*, (1990) 101.

10. Lennard, *op.cit*.154-165, David Calvert, *The history of Herstmonceux Castle*, (undated, c.1984) 8-13.

11. For the Dacre family, *The complete peerage*, (1916); Lennard,*op.cit*.,57-8; and the Barrett Lennard papers in the Essex County Record Office.

12. *Ibid* 170. Several different notations are used for the Dacre barons: Lucas counts from the beginning of the barony in the early 14th century, others (including Lennard) start a new series for the 'Dacres of the South' beginning with Richard Fiennes in 1458. *The complete peerage* uses a third version. Gregory Fiennes (1541-1594) is there referred to as the Xth Lord Dacre, while in Lucas he is the 19th, and in Lennard the 4th.

13. Lucas 3-4. For a review of the literature, Helen M. Lyle, *The rebellion of Jack Cade 1450* (1950); for a recent study, I.M.W.Harvey*, op.cit.*

Chapter 4. BAYLEY WOOD AND BAYLEY PARK: THE LENNARDS

1. For the Wealden iron industry, see H.Cleere and D. Crossley, *The iron industry of the Weald*, (1985) and the earlier pioneer study by Ernest Straker, *Wealden iron*, (1931). For a short account, J.R. Armstrong, *A history of Sussex*, (1974) ch. xvi. For references to the Fiennes brass in Heathfield church, T.W. Horsfield, *The history, antiquities and topography of the county of Sussex*, (1835) vol I, 577; M.A. Lower, *History of Sussex*, (1870) 227; SNQ, vol 1 (1926-7) 151; A.G. Sadler, *The lost monumental brasses of Sussex*, (1988) 97.

2. Calvert, *op.cit*.15

3. J.H. Baker (ed), *The reports of Sir John Spelman*, (1978) vol II,140,200. In 1535 new legislation, 'the Statute of Uses', was passed to prohibit the practices which had grown up.

4. Dacre entry in *DNB*; Lucas 45.

5. Lennard, *op.cit*.207-224.

6. Cleere & Crossley, *op.cit.* ch 7; C.E. Brent, 'Rural employment and population in Sussex between 1550 and 1640' in SAC, vol 114, 30-31.

7. Lucas 44.

8. Lucas 35-6. The Manor of Heathfield later passed into the hands of the de la Warr family. All that remains of it now is the honorific title of Lord of the Manor.

9. M.Clough, 'The estates of the Pelham family in east Sussex before 1500', (1956: unpublished Ph.D thesis) 14-18,30-41; Lucas 44.

10. Lucas 45. The reference to Burwash was almost certainly to the Manor rather than the place.

11. For details of the living standards and social life of the Dacres, see Anthony Fletcher, *A county community in peace and war: Sussex 1600-1660*, (1975) ch.2. Also John E. Ray, 'The parish church of All Saints, Herstmonceux, and the Dacre tomb' SAC vol 58 (1916) 64; Lennard, *op.cit*. 215-228.

12. Lennard, *op.cit*. 226.

13. Lucas 45-6.

14. VCH, vol IX, 205. 'A park of 150 acres was part of the Sapperton estate in 1387 and no doubt formed the nucleus of the present Heathfield Park'. J.L.M Gulley, 'The Wealden landscape in the seventeenth century and its antecedents' (unpublished Ph.D thesis, London, 1960) includes Heathfield in a list of parks recorded before 1300, and Brandon and Short, *op.cit*. 71 suggest that there may have been a medieval park because of the unmodified plant habitat to be found in the present park.

15. PRO STAC 8/197/1.

16. Evelyn quotation in Lucas 48; M.A.Lower, *op.cit*. vol I, 226.

17. Lucas 15-16 describes the commemorative brass plate which was fixed to the gravestone of Catherine Lennard, including its inscription which gave details of her parents and their family tree. He also recounts that in 1740 the then Lord Dacre sought a copy of it from the Vicar of Heathfield.

18. Lennard, *op.cit*. 259, 267-294; Lucas 46-47.

19. For the reference to Lord Dacre's brother, Fletcher, *op.cit*. 28 & 372, note 47. For text of letter, Lucas 47.

20. Lennard, *op.cit*. 285-6; Lucas 48.

21. Lennard, *Ibid* 305-12.

22. *Ibid* 305-330.

23. Ray, *op.cit*. 64, Lennard, *op.cit*. 215-228; ESRO ACC 5281/962 Box 2. Abstract of Deed.

CHAPTER 5. THE NEW OWNERS

1. Anthony Fletcher, *A county community in peace and war. Sussex 1600-1660*, (1975) 27; SAC, vol. xx (1863) 232; VCH vol.II, 297-8; Brandon (74) 171.

2. Fletcher, *op.cit*. 42-3.

3. Celia Fiennes, *The journeys of Celia Fiennes*, (1983 ed.) 154.

4. Ibid.

5 Cleere & Crossley, *op.cit*. 166,180,187,198.

6. In the schedule of deeds in ESRO ACC 5281/962 he is 'Powlett'; Lucas 48 prefers 'Pawlett' and refers only to the purchase of 117 acres of the park.

7. ESRO ASH 160. Transcript 59a. This letter is not dated or signed, but clearly refers to Bayley. It may have been written in late 1674, but more likely after the initial sale to Powlett.

8. ESRO ACC 5281/962. Box 2 Document dated 18 January 1675.

9. Lucas 48-50 gives details about Plummer's varying fortunes from the records of the Worshipful Company of Painters and Stainers. It is possible that the Elizabeth Plomer who in 1655 married William Wilkin, Vicar of Heathfield, was a relative.

10. Ibid 48-49. ESRO ACC 5281/962 Box 2

for document dated 30 October 1682 in which Turvin agreed to provide Plummer with a mortgage of £500 on the Park and 'the Mansion House lately erected'. The painting attributed to van Edema, a large oil measuring 129.5 x 148.5cm entitled *A view of Old Heathfield Hall, Sussex* was offered for sale by Sotheby's on 10 April 1991 and later sold by Lane Fine Art, New Bond Street. Previous owners include two former Heathfield residents, Millicent Thompson and Gordon Langley Hall (now Dawn Langley Simmons. See her autobiography, *Dawn. A Charleston legend* (1995).

11. Lucas 11 & 48-50; ESRO ACC 5281/962 Box 2 for documents giving details of Turvin's loans to Plummer. Jane Plummer, one of his daughters, married John Seavenock of Heathfield on 21 April 1693 in London. SNQ, vol 2, 234. They and their son were subsequently buried in Heathfield church.

12. ESRO ACC 5281/962 for Fuller purchase: Abstract of deed dated 21 June 1708. Lucas 50 quotes a figure of £990.

13. Lucas 50 & 72.

14. Cleere and Crossley, *op.cit.* 190-5, Lucas 88-8.

15. David Crossley and Richard Savile (eds), *The Fuller letters 1728-1755. Guns, slaves and finance.* SRC vol 76 (1991) xviii; VCH vol. IX, 201. See also Lucas 74-75 for the covenants John Fuller negotiated in April 1698 to establish his drawing rights of water going through Twissell and Hamm Mill, located between Bayley Park and the

New Furnace.

16. *Fuller Letters* xxiv; M.A.Lower, *op.cit.* vol 1,226.

17. ESRO SAS RF 3/95. This document calls it 'Bayles' House and Park. The Banqueting House was probably one of the pavilions adjacent to the Plummer mansion.

18. Lucas 51, quoting Sylvan Harmer's account.

19. Ibid 121-2.

20. *Fuller Letters*, no 356 to Richard Allen and Mrs Ann Lade. For Lade's loan to Blackmore, see ESRO ACC 2581/962 Box 2. Abstract of agreement dated 21 February 1739.

21. ESRO *Ibid* for abstract of sale agreement. (This contradicts Lucas 51 who puts the date of sale two years earlier); Box 1 for abstract of agreement concluded on 25 March 1741 by John Blackmore and two of his brother's creditors, members of the Middle Temple.

22. Lucas 51-3 who elaborates on his Royal descent; Algernon Greaves, *Westminster Abbey registers*, (1876) 389; Sir Bernard Burke, *The general armoury*, (1884), entry for O'Keeffe.

23. ESRO ACC 5282/962 Box 1.

24. *Fuller Letters*, no 462, 4 March 1742/3. Lucas 51.

25. Lucas 52; Greaves, *op.cit.* 401.

26. Lucas 52-3; ESRO, Ibid.

Chapter 6. THE WAR HERO: GENERAL GEORGE ELIOTT

1. For biographical details of General George Eliott (1st Lord Heathfield), see *Dictionary of National Biography*; Lucas 53-55; T.H.McGuffie, *The siege of Gibraltar 1779-83*, (1965); Jack Russell, *Gibraltar besieged, 1779-1783*, (1965).

2. Russell, *op.cit.* 35.

3. For examples of Fuller's difficulties, see

Crossley and Saville (eds), *The Fuller Letters, 1728-1755* (1991). For quotation from Horace Walpole, Brandon and Short, op.cit. 247.

4. ESRO ACC 5281/962, Abstract of Title, 18 July 1766.

5. Lucas 53-4.

6. Lucas 53 & 111; ESRO ACC 5281/962

Bayley Park 1791 sale particulars for details of estate.

7. This quotation comes from notes made by the late Col. G.Ll Humphreys, a former president of the Heathfield local history group: I have not been able to trace the original source.

8. Lucas 111; *Historical Associations of the old Independent Chapel, Heathfield, Sussex, 1769-1919.* (1919) 1-6; James Paul, *The Christian soldier. A memoir of the Revd George Gilbert by a friend*, (1833).

9. Russell 5; McGuffie 25. In the following account of the siege, I have drawn heavily on both these books, as well as John Drinkwater's earlier and classic account, *A history of the late siege of Gibraltar*, (1785). ESRO RAF/F/13/8 for Eliott's 1781 Log book.

10. This version is given in Russell 7.

McGuffie 46 has two other versions, only one of which ascribes a role to Mrs Skinner, wife of an officer in the Soldier Artificer Company. Another asserts that it was a military band which played 'Britons strike home' rather than Eliott declaiming the words.

11. Russell 5 & 121.

12. *Ibid* 199-200

13. *Ibid* 273-4.

14. McGuffie 189-190; Russell 275-6.

15. Russell 36 for the description of Lord Heathfield by Sir Gilbert Elliot.

16. Lucas 54; ESRO PAR 372/1/1/3 for dates of baptism.

17. *The Times*, 11 February 1989.

18. ESRO ACC 5281/962. Box 1.

Chapter 7. THE ESTATE IN ITS HEYDAY: FRANCIS NEWBERY

1. Peter Brandon, *The Sussex landscape* (1974) ch.6; ESRO SAS/RF 15/21 for John Fuller's Crop Book for the Heathfield estate (1781-90).

2. Brian M.Short, 'The changing rural society and economy of Sussex 1750-1945' in *Sussex: Environment, landscape and society.* (University of Sussex, 1983) 153-157.

3. Brandon, *Sussex landscape, 178-183.*

4. ESRO ACC 5281/962 Box 1. Sale particulars, 1791.

5. ESRO *Ibid* for details of Newbery's purchase; Lucas 56 for dates recorded in Mrs Newbery's diary; Lucas 26-8 for Richard Wilkin. On his death Wilkin left a collection of his books for the use of the vicars of Heathfield. They were kept in the Old Vicarage for many years: they are now housed at Chichester Cathedral.

6. Biographical details of Francis Newbery (including a fragment of autobiography) and his father are given in Charles Welsh, *A bookseller of the last century* (1885).

7. *Ibid* 36

8. *Ibid* 120.

9. For more on James Fever Powder, including the dispute about its origins, see DNB entry for Robert James MD. For Newbery's defence see *The Morning Post* 7 April 1774.

10. Welsh, *op.cit.* 144-5.

11. For building of Gibraltar Tower, Horsfield, *op.cit.* vol I,575; Lucas 66-68.

12. ESRO AMS 6310, Repton's 'Red Book', purchased in 1993. The version quoted in Lucas 58-9 differs in detail, though not in spirit, and is taken from another of Repton's works, *Observations on the theory and practice of landscape gardening* (1803) 72-3.

13. For the follow-up to Repton's proposals, see Lucas 60; ESRO ACC 5281/962 Box 1 for Newbery exercise book (undated) giving details of Tower plantation, and AMS 6080/3 William Figg's 1819 map of the Heathfield Estate. For the relevance of

Repton's views to recent planning disputes, Nigel F. Marshall, 'Evidence on landscape issues' presented to Public Inquiry on Heathfield Park, 7 July 1992, para 3.5: 'It is a mark of the genius of Repton that he recognised and put into words what has taken the community almost 200 years to do in the form of the Area of Outstanding Natural Beauty (AONB)'.

14. ESRO ACC 5281/962. Sale particulars, 1819.

15. Lucas 86-7 and 91-5.

16. W.T. Prideaux, *A list of the wardens, members of the Court of Assistants and liverymen of the Worshipful Company of Goldsmiths since 1688* (1936) 19 and 79; Welsh, *op.cit.* 147.

17. Welsh, *op.cit.* 152

18. *Ibid* 148-155.

19. Lucas 62-3.

20. There is only rather fragmentary information about Newbery's later years: his published autobiographical notes end in the early part of his year as Sheriff in 1795.

21. Lucas 60-2.

22. Iolo Williams, *op.cit.* 238. I am grateful to John Bleach of the Sussex Archaeological Society for drawing my attention to this reference. Williams did not make the connection with Newbery and the Park, but this is clear from the reference to the 'classical colonnade' of the house.

23. ESRO AMS 6312 for a list of watercolours by William Newbery in two albums sold by Sothebys in 1991-93, and subsequently broken up and dispersed.

24. Eric Shanes, *Turner's England 1810-38* (1990) 8.

25 *Ibid* 29 reproduces and comments on the 'Vale of Heathfield' watercolour, calling it 'this splendid drawing'. Turner's 'Vale of Heathfield sketchbook' containing a pencil drawing on which the painting was based is now in the Clore Gallery at the Tate.

26 *Ibid* 8-10 for details of the vicissitudes of the project to publish a series of 'Views in Sussex'.

27. Lucas 17 for text of inscription on the Newbery family tomb.

Chapter 8. THE IMPERIAL CONNECTION: THE BLUNTS

1. For biographical details and financial activities of Sir John Blunt 1st Bt., John Carswell, *The South Sea Bubble* (1960).

2. Carswell, *op.cit.* 275.

3. P.J. Marshall. *East Indian fortunes. The British in Bengal in the 18th century* (1976) esp. chps I, VII and VIII.

4. For biographical details of Sir Charles William Blunt 3rd Bt., *Gentleman's Magazine* (1803) 283.

5. For biographical details of Sir Charles Richard Blunt 4th Bt., Burke's Peerage; Cockayne, *The complete Baronetage*; Lucas 64; *Gentleman's Magazine* (1840) 430, and *History of Parliament, 1820-1832* (in preparation).

6. ESRO ACC 5281/962 (Box 1) for details of the 1819/20 sale, and the disputes arising from it.

7. John Lowerson, *A short history of Sussex* (1980) 123-8 & Brandon and Short, *The South East from AD 1000* (1990) 234-5 for economic and social conditions after the Napoleonic wars.

8. Lucas, ch XIII 'The workhouse and the poor of the parish'.

9. For the 'Captain Swing' riots of 1830, E.J. Hobsbaum and George Rudé, *Captain Swing* (1969) and Lowerson, *op.cit.* 128-140. For the Heathfield area, Lucas 147-8.

10. For the reform movement in Lewes, John Phillips, 'Partisan behaviour in adversity: voters in Lewes during the Reform era', *Parliamentary History*, (1987) vol 6, pt 2.

11. For early 19th c politics in Lewes, Colin Brent, *Georgian Lewes,1714-1830* (1993), chs 9 & 10; W.H. Hills, *The parliamentary history of the borough of Lewes 1295-1885* (1908) ; and W.D. Cooper, 'Parliamentary History' in T.W. Horsfield, *The history, antiquities and topography of the county of Sussex*, (1835), vol II, Appendix III. For the 1831 election campaign, *Sussex Advertiser*, 28 March; 4, 11,18, 25 April; 2 May 1831.

12. *Sussex Advertiser* 9 May 1831; W.H. Wills, *op.cit.* 37-9.

13. *Sussex Agricultural Express* 1 July 1837.

14. *Ibid* 29 July 1837.

15. Lucas, 65.

16. Heathfield Estate account books, 1837-39, 1840-44, 1845-47 (Private source).

17. Simon Lamb, 'Brief life – Sir Walter Blunt', *Watercolours and Drawings* Winter 1989; Lucas 64; *Gentleman's Magazine* (1847) 333.

18. *Sussex Express* 30 April 1859; 1861 Census.

19. Lucas 65, footnote.

20. Sworn Declaration, 30 September 1891, by John Edmund Brand (Private source).

21. For accounts of the 1859 parliamentary election in Lewes, *Sussex Express* April 19 & 30, May 3 & 28 1859.

22. Kelly's *Brighton Directory* 1882. For Heathfield school, ESRO PAR 372/25/1/1.

23. Brandon and Short, 323; Kelly's *Sussex Directory*, 1862.

24. Brandon and Short, 327-8.

25. Kelly's *Brighton Directory*, 1870; *All Saints Parish Church, Old Heathfield* (1977).

26. J.H. Turner, *The London, Brighton and South Coast Railway*, 3 vols, (1977-9) esp. vol II, 31,151-172, 272-3, vol III 3-11; V. Mitchell and Keith Sutton, *Southern main lines: Tonbridge to Hastings* (1987); A.C. Elliott, *The Cuckoo line* (1988).

27. J.H. Turner, *op.cit.* 31.

28. Quoted in Elliott, *op.cit.* 6

29. Elizabeth Doff, 'A study of Heathfield, 1880-1910. The evolution of a Wealden railway town', *Sussex History*, October 1976.

30. ESRO P 372/2/1. Minutes of Heathfield Parish Council, 21 January 1898; *Sussex Express* 5 January 1895.

31. *Sussex Express* 10 April 1880.

32. *Ibid* 8 and 15 Nov 1890.

33. *Ibid* 15 August 1891.

Chapter 9. HEATHFIELD EXPANDS: THE ESTATE CONTRACTS

1. Quoted in Brandon and Short, *op.cit.* 356. For Wealden gardens created at this time, Shirley Nicholson, *Nymans. The story of a Sussex garden.* (1992). For a list of the most prominent country houses in the county at the time, *Deacon's Court Guide and County Blue Book*, 1894, 156-169.

2. Alan Gillet and Barry K Russell, *Around Heathfield in old photographs* (1990) 7-9;

3. Elizabeth Doff, *op.cit.*

4. For details of the growth of the town, V.M. Taylor, *Heathfield. The growth of the High Street.* (1982) and *Heathfield. The railway and after. A century of change.* (1984).

5. ESRO P 372/2/1. Heathfield Parish Council minutes, 17 January & 18 July 1899.

6. ESRO, *Ibid.* For protests about under-representation, 15 July & 2 October 1902; for protests about neglect of roads, 15 January 1907, 19 January 1909, 19 July 1910, 17 January 1911.

7. John Weller, *One church, one faith, one Lord. A short history of the Union Church Heathfield.* (1979).

8. For biographical details of F.H. Scott, *Sussex Express,* 13 September 1918 and *Centenary brochure,* Heathfield Park cricket club (1978).

9. *Sussex Express* 29 November 1890.

10. *Sussex Express* 15 August 1891.

11. For biographical details of W.C. Alexander, *Who was Who 1916-1928, Sussex Express* 21, 28 April & 5 May 1916. For his will, *Ibid* 8 September 1916.

12. E.R. and J. Pennell, *The life of James McNeill Whistler* vol.1 (1909) 172-5.

13. Gavin Stamp and André Goulancourt, *The English house, 1860-1914* (1986) 233. See also Richard A Fellow, *Sir Reginald Blomfield. An Edwardian architect* (1985).

14. Ian Nairn and Nikolaus Pevsner, *The buildings of England, Sussex* (1965) 531; Clive Aslett, *The last country houses* (1982) 319; Lucas 65; *The Builder* 16 February 1898, 108-9.

15. ESRO ACC 6258. The cutting from the *Sussex Express* is undated, but probably belongs to the period 1908-11.

16. *Sussex Express* 8 January 1909.

17. *Sussex Express* 4 September 1897.

18. *Sussex Express* 21 April & 5 May 1916.

19. For wartime concerts, *Sussex Express* 12 & 19 May and 17 Nov 1916: for local eco-

nomic impact of the war, 27 December 1918.

20. 'Strolling in Sussex', *Courier* 26 May 1978. This occasional series by 'Harry Hobden' (the late Ray Deadman) is a mine of local information.

21. ESRO P 372/2/3. Heathfield parish council minutes, 1928-40. 9 July & 8 October 1935, 14 January 1936.

22. *Ibid* 7 April 1932.

23. *Ibid* 15 February 1933, 9 January 1934.

24. For biographical details of James Groves, *Sussex Express* 18 January 1935. Additional information from local interviews.

25. ESRO P 372/2/3. Heathfield parish council minutes 15 November 1928. In making the gift, Mr Groves wrote: 'I would like to stipulate that it be kept an open space in perpetuity'. The council agreed unanimously to accept the gift 'on the terms of his letter'.

26. ESRO AMS 5837/1. Heathfield Park sale particulars, 1935.

27. For biographical details of Harry Clifford-Turner, and the history of his firm – on which I have drawn heavily - John Scott, *Legibus. A history of Clifford-Turner 1900-1980* (1980).

28. Scott, *op.cit.* 96-100.

29. *Ibid* 76.

Chapter 10. WORLD WAR II

1. Information on the local Home Guard provided by Raymond Neave and Harry Parsons. Limited documentation is to be found in ESRO HGD files. Also PRO WO 166/6044 27 March 1942 for structure of East Sussex Group.

2. For the origins, development and organisation of the Auxiliary Units, David Lampe, *The last ditch* (1968).

3. *Ibid* 131; Charles A Robertson, *Hailsham and its environs* (1982) 214-5 Appendix R; R.A. Elliston, *Lewes at war 1939-1945*

(1995) 107-9; *Sunday Telegraph*, 3 July 1994 'Britain's secret resistance group gathers again'. The location in Heathfield Park has been confirmed by Winifred Read.

4. ESRO SHE 2/7/808.

5. Details of troop movements in and out of the Park are to be found in the War Diaries and Situation Reports of South-Eastern Command in PRO WO 166. Some of the records for individual British units are also there, including those of HQ 55 Div. (PRO WO 166/689). For the Canadian troops,

C.P. Stacey, *Six years of war. Official history of the Canadian army in the second world war*, vol 1 (1955) especially 279-9; and C.P. Stacey and Barbara M Wilson, *The half-million. The Canadians in Britain 1939-46* (1987) esp.16.

6. For Montgomery and his relations with the Canadians, Nigel Hamilton, *Monty. The making of a general 1887-1942* (1981) esp. 496-555.

7. PRO WO 166/140 and eye-witness account by Syd Hopkins.

8. Hamilton, *op.cit.* 506-7.

9. Ronald Atkin, *Dieppe 1942, The Jubilee disaster* (1980) 17; Stacey and Wilson, *op.cit.16.*

10. Hamilton, *op.cit.* 555.

11. Atkin, *op.cit.* 16-21.

12. General Sir Allan Adair, *A Guard's General.* (1986) 136; PRO WO 166/14191 for location of units in Heathfield.

13. Lt. Col. Lord Birdwood, *The Worcestershire Regiment* (1952) 47-52.

14. Adair, *op.cit.* 136-159.

Chapter 11. A CHANGED WORLD

1.H.A. Clemenson, *English country houses and landed estates,* (1981) 138-9; James Lees-Milne, *People and places,* (1992); Simon Jenkins, 'The noblest nationalisation', *The National Trust Magazine*, Spring 1995, 45-6.

2. Information on 1947 sale price from the late Reginald Clifford-Turner.

3. Biographical details of Sir John Harvey Blunt, 9th Bt., *Burke's Peerage and Baronetage*, 1949; for the Aga Khan's gift, Sotheby's Heathfield Park sale catalogue 19 May 1993, no 393.

4. For biographical details of Sir John Blunt, 10th Bt., *Who's Who* 1966, *Sussex Express*, 10 October 1969. For Margaret, Lady Blunt, *Debrett* 1971.

5. For the history of the family, Cecil Roth, *The Sassoon Dynasty* (1941).

6.*Ibid* ch. ix.

7.*Ibid* 204-16; James Knox, 'Not our gods. Philip Sassoon at 25 Park Lane', *Country Life* 17 November 1994.

8. Roth, *op.cit.* 222.

9. Heathfield Park sale particulars,1963.

10. Sussex Rural Community Council, *Tomorrow in Sussex* (undated, c.1946)

11. (Old) Heathfield Womens' Institute Scrapbook, 1952.

12 'Strolling in Sussex', *Courier* 9 March 1979.

13. *Sussex County Magazine* vol 12 (1938) 154. Hailsham RDC thought the choice of site and design by the County Council to be 'deplorable'. For post-war developments see *Sussex Express* 23 July and 22 October 1948 and 14 January 1949.

14. The Village Institute at Cade Street was built in 1906 by Mr Alexander, and donated with the land by his daughter Mrs Grace Lister in September 1921. The Goward Hall was added in 1937/8 by Mr E A Goward on land donated by Mr Clifford-Turner. *Sussex Express* 20 February 1948. and 30 September 1949. For the State Hall, see 'Strolling in Sussex', *Courier* 25 August 1978.

15. 'Strolling in Sussex', *Courier* 26 May 1978; A.C. Elliott, *The Cuckoo Line*, 139.

16. Planning applications K/63/1400-4 submitted on 30 October 1963, and K/63/1437 submitted on 29 October 1963. For the grant of land, made on 13 September 1964, *Heathfield Park Cricket Club centenary brochure* (1978) 28.

17. The title *Treading in treacle* arose from Gerald Moore's early love of long and unfamiliar words. One day at school 'At the end of one lesson an angry, exasperated Mr Harnett pronounced his verdict on my prospects: "You'll be treading in treacle all your life, Moore" *Op.cit.* 82.

18. *Ibid*,11.

19. Sotheby's Heathfield Park sale catalogue, 19 May 1993. Foreword by Dr Gerald Moore.

20. *Treading in treacle*, 262, 295-7

21. Sotheby's sale catalogue, 1993, Foreword.

22. *Sunday Mirror* 9 February 1969, *Evening News* 6 June 1969, *Daily Mirror* 7 June 1969, *Sun* 4 June 1970. *Daily Telegraph* 26 November 1970 ('Disciplinary case against doctor closed'). Dr Moore subsequently won an apology and damages in a libel action against News of the World Ltd for an article in the *Sun*: *Daily Telegraph* 12 February 1971, *Sun* 28 April 1970 and 15 February 1971. The *Sun* 26 July 1969 had previously had to apologise for another inaccurate article about Dr Moore.

23. *Daily Telegraph* 30 November 1970.

24. *Sussex Express* 23 September 1977 for Dr Moore's evidence to public inquiry about initial public dissatisfaction. For the Wheeler statues, *Evening News* (London) 22 October 1973 'Home in the country for male nudes'.

25. *Sussex Express* 23 September and 7 October 1977. At the 1977 public inquiry a figure of 300,000 visitors over four years was quoted.

26. For escapes of animals, *Courier* 15 September 1978, *Sussex Express* 22 June 1979.

27. For a summary of the planning history of the Wildlife Park, as well as later developments, see 'Proof of Evidence... on behalf of Wealden District Council by Mr I M Kay, Assistant District Planning Officer', Public Inquiry about Heathfield Park, Crowborough July 1992. (Doc. WD. AP 189326/1).

28. *News of the World* 26 August 1973 & 11 September 1977, 'A perilous walk on the wildside at the Doc's zoo'.

29. *Sussex Express* 21 September 1979 for closure of Wildlife Park; *West Sussex Gazette*

20 March 1980 for announcement of sale to take place on Thursday 3 April.

30. For more on these designations, and the ecology of the Park, see 'Evidence on landscape issues' (and Appendices) presented by Nigel F. Marshall to the Public Inquiry held at Crowborough on 7 July 1992, and 'Heathfield Park landscape report' by Chris Blandford Associates, presented on the same occasion.

31. Planning application WD/79/770/R. At one stage in the negotiations, a safari park was mooted: *Sussex Express* 8 June 1979. 'Coming soon - the lions of Heathfield. Wildlife Park to go safari-style?'

32. *Sussex Express* 5 June, 3 & 31 July, 16 October 1981; 19 March, 23 April, 11 June 1982; *Courier* 3 June, 2 August, 16 & 23 October, 13 November 1981; 18 June 1982.

33. *Courier* 3 December 1984 & 19 April 1985.

34. Land Registry transfer, 2 September 1987.

35. *Courier* and *Sussex Express* 23 October 1987 and 2 February 1990.

36. *Ibid*, 14 December 1990. See also 'Heathfield Park (West). A discussion document and outline proposals'. Dunthorne Parker, September 1990, and an (undated) pamphlet issued by them for the public viewing in February 1991.

37. Ian Kay, *'Proof of Evidence'*, July 1992, paras 60-161.

38. Letter from Department of the Environment to Wealden D.C. 12 February 1993.

39. Sale particulars, Knight Frank & Rutley: advertisement on opening page of *Country Life* 18 March 1993.

40. The BBC programme, in a series called 'Auction', was transmitted on 9 February 1994.

Chapter 12. THE PARK TODAY: A FAMILY HOME AGAIN

1. *Sunday Telegraph* 10 October 1993. 'Fast Viking heads for the market' by Judi Bevan.

2. Jill Berg, *The Offshore Grand Prix: There's no turning back.* (1994)

3. The High Court hearing took place before the Queen's Bench Division on 2 December 1993. For the decision of the Secretary of State, *Sussex Express* and *Courier* 31 March 1995.

ILLUSTRATIONS: ACKNOWLEDGMENTS

I am grateful to the private owners of the following paintings for permission to reproduce them:

Heathfield Old Hall, attrib. Gerard van Edema. (Photo Lane Fine Art); *Sir Walter Blunt* by Alfred Edward Chalon, R.A. (Photo by courtesy of the National Portrait Gallery); *W.C. Alexander* by Philip Connard. (Photo Courtald Institute of Art).

Acknowledgments are also due to the following galleries and museums:

By permission of the British Library: pp. 29, 30, 31, 35, 36 (9904.r.5); pp. 78 and 80 (11899.666.22).
Copyright, British Museum: pp. 61, 64, 69, 97, see also colour section.
By kind permission of the East Sussex County Archivist: pp. 5, 83, 84, 85, 88 and colour section; and Adams and Remers: pp. 76, 95 and 100.
By permission, Imperial War Museum: p. 147.
By courtesy of the Trustees, The National Gallery, London: p. 50.
By courtesy of the National Portrait Gallery: p. 62.
From the collection of the Sussex Archaeological Society: pp. 21, 22, 39, 43, 81.
By courtesy of the Trustees, The Tate Gallery: p. 127.
By permission of the Dean and Chapter of Westminster: p. 48
Illustrations on pp. 28, 34, 41, 56 and 79 are from *Heathfield Memorials*, and on pp. 138 and 140 from John Scott, *Legibus, A history of Clifford-Turner, 1900-1980*.

INDEX